THE MA

Calvin as a young man

THE MAN OF GENEVA

The Story of John Calvin

by

Elsie M. Johnson

THE BANNER OF TRUTH TRUST

THE BANNER OF TRUTH TRUST
3 Murrayfield Road, Edinburgh EH12 6EL
PO Box 621, Carlisle, Pennsylvania 17013, USA

*

© The Banner of Truth Trust
First published 1977

ISBN 0 85151 254 2

*

Printed in Great Britain by
Hazell Watson & Viney Ltd, Aylesbury, Bucks

CONTENTS

1	John Goes to Paris	9
2	New Ideas	20
3	The Hunted Man	30
4	They Met in Secret	39
5	Adventures in Italy	48
6	The City on the Lake	58
7	Contending with the Councils	67
8	Banished from Geneva	78
9	Calvin and the Cardinal	90
10	Geneva Calls Again	99
11	Calvin's Growing Influence	109
12	The Crowning Joy	120

ILLUSTRATIONS

Calvin as a young man	*Frontispiece*
Calvin's home in the Cornmarket Square, Noyon	11
General View of old Paris	14
Collège de Montaigu	16
Jacques Lefèvre lecturing at the Sorbonne	22
Cathedral of Notre Dame, Paris (18th Century)	32
Calvin 'welcomed into the homes of the poor'	40
Farel preaching in the open-air	54
Geneva (17th Century)	60
View in the Alps	68
Calvin threatened, a Scene in the Church at Rive in 1538	80
Cathedral of Strasburg	97
Calvin re-enters Geneva	102
Cardinal Sadoleto visits Calvin	106
Calvin and Servetus before the Council	112
Calvin preaching in the Cathedral of St. Pierre	118
Addressing the Council for the last time	126

I
JOHN GOES TO PARIS

'Off to Paris at last!' exclaimed fourteen-year-old John, as he threw his cap into the air in sheer excitement.

'Yes, it's true, we are really on the way,' agreed his companions with equal enthusiasm.

It was a lovely summer morning in the year 1523, when John Calvin, with the two Montmor boys and his special friend Claude de Hangest, set off for the great city. They rode on horseback and had an escort, for in those days it was not safe to travel alone. Highwaymen would be lying in wait for any rash travellers who appeared to be unarmed and without a bodyguard. The boys, however, had no fears. There were too many things to keep them excited on the sixty-mile journey. Sometimes they would urge their horses into a gallop to see who would be first at a given point. Occasionally, they would come almost to a halt, as they bombarded their tutors with questions about the places through which they were passing.

Soon their native town of Noyon was left far behind. Noyon was an old cathedral city in the province of Picardy, with strong walls to keep out its enemies. It had a famous Bishop, who was also its ruler. The life of the city centred around the

THE MAN OF GENEVA

Church. Priests and monks in their long, dark robes were everywhere, and people came from far and near to see the carefully preserved relics of the saints.

With a population of ten thousand, Noyon was also a trading centre for the surrounding villages. Donkeys laden with sacks of flour – their owners bargaining for the highest prices – could often be seen in the old Cornmarket Square.

That summer, however, the inhabitants of Noyon were afraid. People were dying. The plague had struck once more. It was just as well that the boys were leaving the disease-infested city, though the real reason for their departure was the higher education which Paris offered.

After a few hours, in order to rest the horses the party put up at a roadside inn. The proprietor immediately gave them his personal attention. It was not every day that he entertained sons of the aristocracy; therefore his guests must be conducted to the best rooms; they must be served with the best food.

The ostler made it his business to see that good fodder and stabling was provided for the steeds.

The arrival of the visitors caused quite a stir among the serving girls, who were all anxious to perform some little duty which might be rewarded with a smile and a silver coin when the travellers left.

Calvin's home in the Cornmarket Square, Noyon

Sitting in a dark corner, an old farmer watched the scene with great interest. He was amazed at the hustle and bustle, and all the fuss. Beckoning the inn-keeper, he enquired in a low voice:

'Who are they, these young gentlemen? Look – that one over there, in the scarlet cloak and woollen hose. He looks a fine handsome youth. Who is he?'

'He is Claude de Hangest, nephew of the Bishop of Noyon,' replied mine host, and then continued, 'The others belong to the same tribe, except that boy in the dark clothes. Son of a church lawyer, he is. They call him Jean Cauvin.'

The old man was still curious.

'What are they doing here? Where are they going?' he questioned.

Fortunately the innkeeper was quite happy to pass on information.

'They are going to Paris to study,' he said, and then added, with a twinkle in his eyes, 'They will be learning how to keep you and me in our proper place!'

The farmer was satisfied. It would be something new to tell his wife when he got home.

The boy in the dark clothes, to whom the inn-keeper had made reference, was of course John Calvin. In speaking to the old farmer, the landlord had used the boy's French name.

John's father, Gérard Cauvin, worked hard in

JOHN GOES TO PARIS

the employment of the Church, and it brought him in touch with important people. John therefore soon became acquainted with the most important families in the district. When members of the distinguished de Hangest family began to take an interest in him, it turned out to be very much to his advantage. The de Hangest mansion became his second home. There he played games, and there in the parkland he learned to ride a horse.

With his friends, John studied under a private tutor, and later he went with them to a boys' school in Noyon. It was called the Collège des Capettes – the college of the little hooded capes.

John was very happy in the company of his wealthy young friends. They were genuinely fond of him. Though they knew his father was not a rich man, they never made him feel poor and inferior.

Arriving at last in the Capital, the boys separated, and John made his way through narrow, twisting streets to the home of his uncle, Richard Calvin, a locksmith by trade.

It was great to be in Paris, with so many new and exciting things to enjoy. Yet in those first days in a strange city, it was natural that John's thoughts should go back to Noyon. He thought about his mother who had died when he was only three years old. Again and again, neighbours

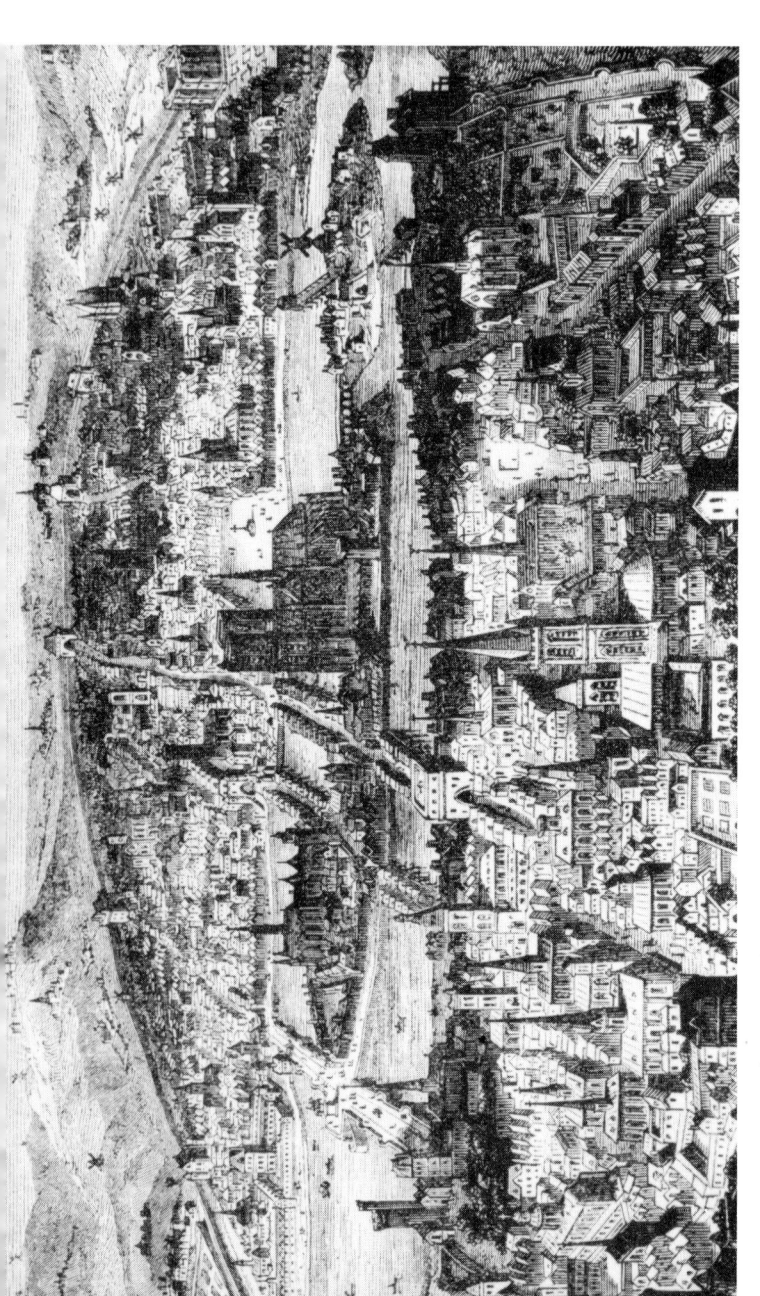

General view of old Paris

had told him how beautiful, and how good she was. He thought also of his step-mother and his brothers and sisters. In particular, he recalled how proud and pleased his father was, to have a son about to enter the university.

The church lawyer always had an eye for his own interests, and the advancement of his sons. From humble beginnings, Gérard Cauvin had managed to push his way up to a higher status in life, and he expected John to do the same. In fact, when John was only twelve years old, his ambitious father had already begun to make plans for his future. Being on good terms with the Bishop, he was able to obtain a junior post for his son in Noyon Cathedral. And so John became a boy chaplain at the altar of La Gésine.

He remembered it clearly, as if it had happened just yesterday. The documents had been signed. His hair had been shaved to leave a bare patch on the crown of his head, according to the rules. It was called a tonsure, and was a sign that he was set apart for the Church.

When he reached home that day, he had been full of questions:

'Father, I didn't understand. What does it really mean?'

'My boy, it is only the first step. It means that one day you will be a priest, and that is what I want for you.'

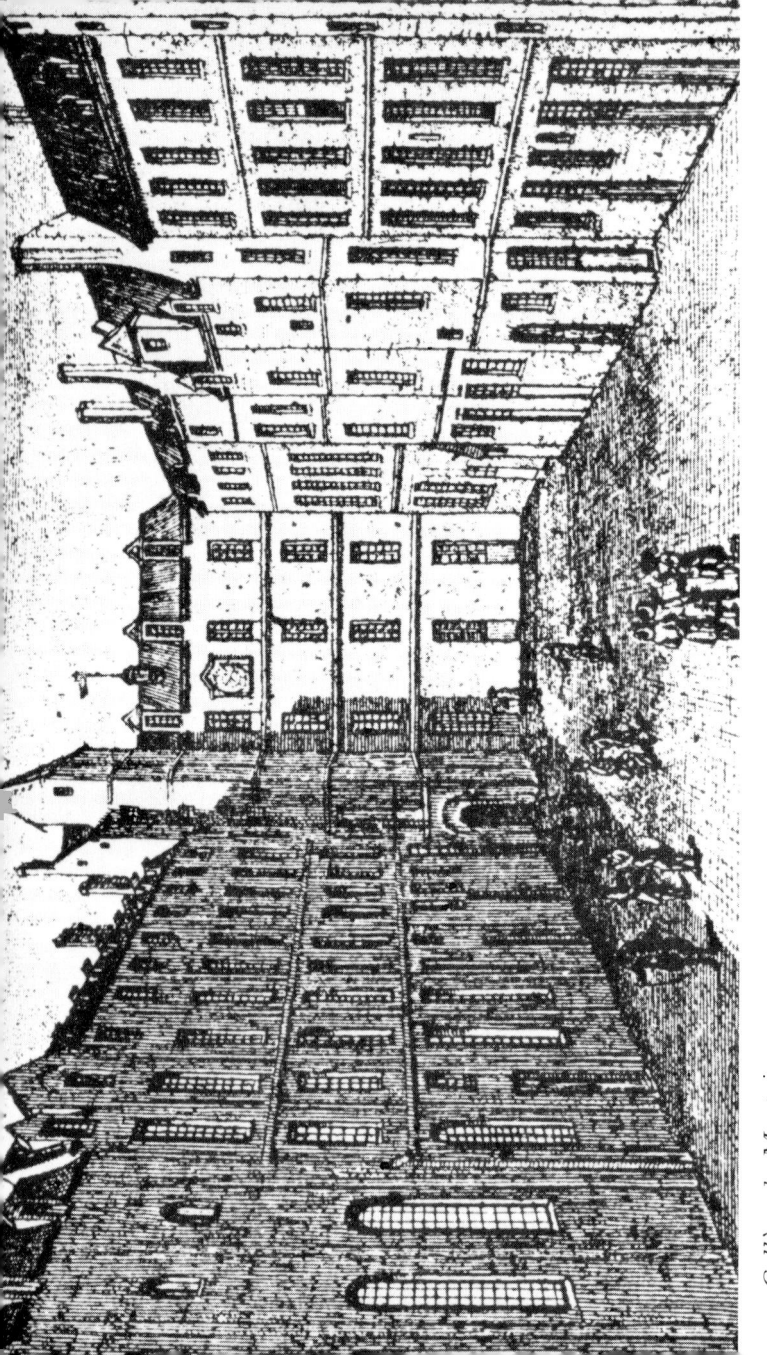

Collège de Montaigu

'But father,' John argued, 'I don't know how to do the work. I could not say the prayers, and I don't know how to speak in Latin.'

'You don't need to be anxious. I will pay a grown-up priest to perform your duties,' John's father replied. Then he added:

'I will only pay him a small sum. Your salary, John, will help with the cost of your future education!'

*

At the University John was in his element. As a new boy at the Collège de la Marche, he was given an excellent grounding in French and Latin. His tutor was the famous Mathurin Cordier, who had more enlightened views on teaching young boys than most schoolmasters of that period! He did not believe in punishment by flogging. His method was to encourage pupils to do well, by offering small prizes.

After a short time John was transferred to the Collège de Montaigu to study theology. It was a dirty, gloomy place with very strict rules, and very poor food. No French was spoken there, only Latin, and woe betide the boy who tried to whisper a word to his neighbour in his mother tongue!

Fortunately, John was determined to succeed in all his lessons. He was not only keen, he was brilliant, and at nineteen, he received the Master of Arts degree.

John soon made the discovery that his world at Noyon had been a very small one. Those walls of his native city had, it seemed, shut out the light of the New Learning which was streaming across Europe. He must find out all about it.

He learned that scholars were going back to study the classical poets and philosophers for their inspiration. They were finding in the ancient Latin and Greek writings the basis for their own new thinking. And, much to his surprise, John found that men of learning were everywhere discussing *the Bible*.

In the year 1516, a former student at the Collège de Montaigu, a Dutchman named Erasmus, had published the Greek New Testament, with a new Latin translation. Its influence was great, and improved editions were continually coming from the printing presses of Basle. In those days the Scriptures were only available to the clergy and scholars, at least, to those who knew Latin. Erasmus said that he wanted to see the Bible translated into every language, so that ordinary people everywhere could read it for themselves.

While Erasmus was praised for his work by many eminent people, the Catholic Church found fault with him and his Greek New Testament.

JOHN GOES TO PARIS

But the real truth was that the Church was afraid of losing its authority. Already the German monk, Martin Luther, had burst upon the scene and had startled Europe by daring to criticize the Pope. Money was needed for the rebuilding of St. Peter's at Rome, and Pope Leo X had authorized monks to go from place to place selling indulgences, or 'letters of pardon,' as Luther once described them.

The great mass of the people were uneducated and superstitious. They were not used to thinking for themselves and they had long been taught that men's souls would have to suffer after death in a place called 'purgatory' before their sins would be pardoned. The Pope's indulgences seemed to offer a much easier way to obtain forgiveness of their sins. So Leo X found that the money flowed in.

Martin Luther declared that the forgiveness of sins could not be bought with money, it was the free gift of God.

But what would young John Calvin think about all this?

II
NEW IDEAS

The entertainments and glittering shows of Paris were a great attraction to young University students and to the fashionable young ladies of the city. John, however, cared little for such things. Making his way one evening to the lodgings of his cousin Robert (Pierre Robert Olivétan), he looked forward to having a long talk with him on the news of the day. They had much in common, for Robert was from Noyon, and like John was in Paris to study. Indeed, Robert often pursued his studies far into the night, and his friends who knew this, nicknamed him 'Olivétan,' meaning 'Midnight Oil.' Eventually, the name given as a joke became his surname.

Bounding up the stairs to his cousin's apartment, John at once made himself at home. The room was poorly furnished, with only a table and a chair, a bed and a bookshelf. A crucifix hung on the wall and a primitive lamp cast an uncertain light on the open book in Robert's hand. John took off his cloak and cap and made himself comfortable at the end of the bed.

'Any news from Noyon?' asked Robert expectantly.

'Sorry, no news this week. I don't get many letters from my father,' was John's reply.

NEW IDEAS

After a while John mentioned something that had been on his mind all the day.

'Robert, will you please tell me about this new faith which seems to be spreading so quickly?'

'Of course,' his cousin answered, 'but really I am surprised at you, John! What have you been hearing to make you ask me about it?'

Robert was three years older than John. He had been won over to the new teaching which soon would be known everywhere as the Protestant faith. Secretly he hoped that John would become a convert, though he was well aware that his cousin was a strong supporter of the Roman Church and its practices.

'Well,' admitted John, 'I have been looking over some of the writings of Jacques Lefèvre. I hear that his New Testament in French has been condemned, and that he has been put out of the Sorbonne.'

John was obviously deeply concerned. The Sorbonne was the Faculty of Theology – or Department of Religion – at Paris, and was very powerful. It was the guardian of the Catholic faith in France, and was responsible to the Pope alone. To be put out, as Lefèvre had been, was very serious indeed.

Robert looked sad as he replied:

'Yes, John, it is true, but who would have thought it possible? Lefèvre was a respected man

Jacques Lefèvre lecturing at the Sorbonne

in the city. He has travelled widely, and is a man of great learning. He must be about seventy years old – it is terrible that this should have happened to him.'

'I suppose the Sorbonne must show its authority,' was all that John could say.

Robert spoke again:

'They can burn Lefèvre's and Luther's books, but nothing can stop the gospel. Do you not know that the Bible has found an entrance into the very palace of the king? Marguerite of Navarre, the king's sister, has accepted a copy from the Bishop of Meaux. Now she is doing what she can to help the preachers.'

John listened, but he was not convinced. He favoured toleration towards the Protestants, and liked to hear all about the new ideas, but he had no intention of following them. He told himself he would become a priest, and a loyal son of the Church, as his father wished.

The cousins talked on and on until the hour was late. Now and again John became angry, especially when Robert began to blame the Church for all the world's miseries. Then young Calvin's eyes flashed, and his voice was raised, as he warned:

'Be careful, Robert, or the Sorbonne will denounce you as a heretic.'

For a moment there was silence. Then Robert quietly answered:

'That may well be; I expect you know that a converted Augustinian monk was burned at the stake for heresy, in the very month you arrived in Paris.'

'Yes, I did hear about it. He was a brave man, and I am sorry they put him to death.'

John's words came slowly, as though he found it hard to speak. And when he said 'Goodnight' and left the house, he found his thoughts turning to Jean Vallière, the monk who had died for his faith at the Place de Grève.

*

The weeks and months passed quickly. John was so busy, there was hardly time for all the things he wanted to do. He did, however, keep in touch with Claude de Hangest, and the Montmors, since being in their company was always enjoyable. He also made many new friends, for his alert mind and love of books brought him to the notice of men of influence. Soon he was welcomed into the circles of the great. The royal Librarian, Guillaume Budé, noted for his specialized knowledge of the Greek language, was one famous man to whom John could look for friendship and guidance. Then there was King Francis' chief physician, Guillaume Cop of Basle, who was not only skilled in medicine, but was also a man of letters, who liked to encourage University students who showed promise. Young Calvin was often invited to his home, and was fascinated by the royal doctor's wealth of learning. Soon John became very much attached to Nicholas Cop, one of the sons, and a lasting friendship developed between the two young men.

*

John was getting on well, and the thought of leaving Paris never once entered his mind. Then the shock came. An important letter from his father arrived. It told him to leave the Capital, and take up the study of Law at the University of Orleans. Gérard Cauvin had changed his mind. Not the priesthood, but the legal profession should be John's goal! The Law offered greater opportunities, and greater rewards, father Cauvin told his son.

A young man usually feels that he should be allowed to make up his own mind about his future. But John obeyed his father's orders without question. He went to Orleans, and gave himself to the new studies. Fortunately, there were quite a number of things that he enjoyed. The rules were not so strict and the staff were more open-minded. Thus students could put forward their own ideas more freely.

There were two men who made a very deep impression upon him during his stay at Orleans.

One was Pierre de l'Estoile, the Professor of Law, whose fame had attracted students from many parts of the world. The other was the German, Melchior Wolmar, under whose tuition John learned the rudiments of Greek within a few months. Wolmar was a staunch supporter of Martin Luther, and was always ready to speak about his Christian beliefs. John was once again challenged by the spiritual dynamic of the new faith.

After a year or so, John's legal studies took him to the University of Bourges. Then came a dramatic change! The keen student was called back to his native Noyon, where his father was lying dangerously ill in the family home. Reaching the bedside just in time, John sought to speak a few words of comfort to the dying man in his last moments.

The final years of Gérard Cauvin's life, had been far from happy. He had been in trouble with the Canons of the Cathedral. They had accused him of mis-managing the winding-up of an estate. It was a business matter, yet Gérard stubbornly refused to let the clergy have the account books. Finally the Cathedral Chapter had excommunicated its church lawyer. So, when he died, his sons had to beg the Church authorities for permission to have him buried in consecrated ground.

All this weighed heavily on John's heart and mind. Could it be true what the Protestants so

NEW IDEAS

often said – that the Church shows no mercy; it is greedy for power and wealth and it oppresses those who fail to keep its rules?

John stayed in Noyon for a month. There were family affairs to settle, and the brothers made sure that the account books were duly surrendered to the Noyon clergy. Charles, the elder brother, enjoyed having long talks with John, for Charles himself had entered the priesthood. But, he too had displeased his superiors, and was in disgrace. Patiently, John listened to his bitter complaints.

One night, the conversation took a new turn. The brothers were discussing the terrible disaster which overtook Rome in 1527, when the armies of Emperor Charles V of the Holy Roman Empire, descended upon the city, scaling the walls, and showing no mercy to the inhabitants.

'Tell me about it, for we were kept very much in the dark here in Noyon. You were in Paris, John. Did you not hear a full account?' said Charles to his brother.

'Most of my news came from students who had friends in Italy,' John explained. 'It seems that Pope Clement VII, though normally a clever diplomat, made a fatal decision when he set himself in opposition to Charles V. The Pope never expected his own holy city to be invaded.'

'I was told it lasted a whole month,' said Charles.

'That's true. The regular troops were reinforced by twenty-thousand unpaid mercenaries, and the slaughter went on for weeks. Hundreds were put to death, others were tortured, and women were shamefully treated. Houses were looted, and burnt to the ground.

'But even more than the dreadful loss of life – all that the Church held sacred was desecrated. In mocking derision, soldiers rode through the streets in the purple and scarlet robes of Pope and Cardinals! The priceless vessels of the Vatican were stolen, and used in drunken revelry. Art treasures were slashed to pieces. The Pope himself was held a prisoner in the Castel San Angelo where he had fled for safety.'

As John finished his recital of the tragic events, it was evident that he was upset. The humiliation which the Church suffered during the Sack of Rome was shared by every true Catholic. Many regarded the disaster as a Divine Judgment for the sins of the past, and were prepared to work for the spiritual recovery of the Church.

*

In those long, summer evenings the brothers debated many vital issues concerning Church and State.

Then came the last night, when Charles started on a personal note:

NEW IDEAS

'John, what will you do now? Our father has been taken from us, so have you made new plans for the future?'

'Yes, Charles. For me, it is not the Church, and it is not the Law. I want to be a scholar, I mean a real scholar. I want to master Greek and Hebrew in the same way I have mastered Latin. I want to delve into ancient manuscripts – to translate, and bring to light their hidden treasures.'

'You can hardly expect to become rich, doing that kind of work!' Charles reminded him.

'I know,' answered John, 'but I shall be happy. A quiet study, and shelves lined with books, together with a good supply of paper and ink, is all I need. Then, of course, just enough food and drink to keep me going, that is my idea of a satisfying life!

'Tomorrow I am going to set off for Paris, but not on horseback. I will trust in providence, and walk the sixty miles.'

III
THE HUNTED MAN

King Francis I had just founded a new type of college in Paris. It was quite independent of the University, and the teaching was entrusted to Royal Readers. These men were experts in their own specialized fields of learning, and famous professors had been invited to join the staff. Students at the college enjoyed complete freedom in their choice of academic courses. John therefore decided to continue with his Greek, and also to take up Hebrew. In addition, he gave every spare moment of his time to writing, for he was hard at work on his first book, and was anxious to complete it.

When the day's lectures were over, John hurried to his sanctum. It was a narrow little room which he had rented, in the dormitory of the Collège Fortet – just one in a row of similar rooms where students lived and worked. Night after night the light burned till past the midnight hour, but John was pleased with his progress, and on April 4th, 1532, his book was published. Dedicated to his friend Claude de Hangest, and written in clear and polished Latin, he had high hopes of its success. It was not a religious book, but a commentary on a treatise which had been written by the Roman philosopher and statesman Seneca, who lived centuries before Calvin, and in the time of the apostle Paul.

Unfortunately, John's expectations of fame and recognition were dashed to the ground. No one seemed interested. Only a few copies were sold. It was most humiliating to the young author. John was very disappointed, but was still undaunted.

*

A brief return to Orleans, and then back to Paris, where Calvin found himself in the centre of stirring events. It was All Saints' Day, 1533, and John's friend Nicholas Cop was at this time Rector of the University of Paris, and it was his duty to deliver the Annual Address to the academics, and others, who had gathered in the Church of the Mathurins. The congregation expected a sermon in praise of the saints and 'Holy Mother Church'. Instead, Cop preached on a text from Christ's Sermon on the Mount, 'Blessed are the poor in spirit . . . '. He incorporated in his message some of the teaching of Erasmus and Luther, whose writings were hated by the Sorbonne. Then he upheld the Bible as the living Word of God, and he talked of God's free mercy to sinners.

The Sorbonne was furious. Messengers were hurriedly sent to the Parlement of Paris, demanding that proceedings should be taken against Cop for heresy.

Cathedral of Notre Dame, Paris (18th Century)

THE HUNTED MAN

The Rector felt sure he could give a satisfactory answer to the charge made against him by his accusers. On the appointed day, therefore, he set out for the palace, wearing his robes of office, and carrying the University seal. He walked in procession with an air of confidence, with the beadles carrying his golden staves.

Suddenly there was a scuffle, and a disturbance, as a voice rang out:

'Rector, Rector! Flee for your life. Parlement will not release you! King Francis cannot save you. Flee for your life, man – Flee!'

It was the voice of a friend who had received secret information.

Cop did not hesitate. In the confusion, he turned into a side street and threw off his cap and robes. A crowd of enthusiastic students surrounded him. In less than an hour he had passed through St. Martin's Gate, and out of Paris. Soon afterwards a reward was offered for his capture, alive or dead – the tempting reward of three hundred crowns.

Within two months, Cop reached Basle, the city which had been his father's home in earlier years. Here he was safe, for Basle lay beyond the frontiers of France.

It was John Calvin's turn next. He was Cop's friend, they said, and it was rumoured that he had helped Cop to write the All Saints' Day sermon. They would get him and punish him. So the bailiffs were sent with instructions to arrest him at any cost. He was in his room when they came. There was a great commotion at the foot of the long, winding, narrow staircase. Then a fellow-student rushed in breathless, to give the warning:

'Hurry, John – you must get out of here! – the police are after you.' As he spoke, the student quickly pulled down the curtains which screened the bed, and twisted them to make a strong rope. While he hustled John into a back room, with a window which overlooked a hidden part of the yard, his friends downstairs managed to harass the bailiffs for a few more seconds, and hinder their advance.

Like a flash John slid down the rope, and ran to the house of a friend who kept a vineyard. Stripping off his scholar's gown he dressed himself in a working man's clothes, and made his escape from the city.

The hunted man lost his books and papers, but he was still free.

John found a refuge in the home of Louis du Tillet, curé of Claix near the city of Angoulême. A gentleman of note, and a Canon of the Cathedral, du Tillet was sympathetic to followers of the reform movement. For safety, John took an assumed name. He mixed freely with the many visitors to du Tillet's big house. He wrote out sermons for overworked clerics, and he made good use of the treasures of du Tillet's library, consisting of some three or four thousand books.

Du Tillet and Calvin were kindred spirits. Thus the wanderer found a happy retreat where he could have real fellowship, and where he could think and pray, and read and study in peace.

After a few months had passed, John felt an urge to visit Lefèvre, the old professor who had moved to Nérac to be under the protection of Queen Marguerite of Navarre. Thus at the court of Marguerite at Nérac, the two men met for the first time. Until then, Calvin had known the professor only by repute, and through his writings. This was a wonderful opportunity, John felt, and he made the most of it. Lefèvre listened to his many questions, and was sympathetic and helpful. John went away, realizing it had been a meeting which he would never forget.

*

From early University days John had mixed with men who believed in the reform movement. They were men whom he could look up to, and whom he could trust.

Yet he himself had remained on the fringe – just an observer, taking a neutral position. Even so, the witness of Olivétan, Wolmar and others to a living faith in Christ, had not been in vain.

Suddenly the light of God's Holy Spirit pierced John Calvin's mind and heart.

'God subdued my stubborn heart . . . and pulled me out of the mire,' he wrote many years later.

He became filled with a new zeal – a burning zeal for God and his word. He felt the power of a divine deliverance from sin. The hand of the Lord was upon him, and a new pathway stretched before him.

John thought much about Lefèvre. The eminent professor had remained in the Church of Rome hoping to see it becoming spiritually renewed, but he had been deeply disappointed. The very Church which he had sought to help now despised and persecuted him.

What would John do? Remain in the Roman Catholic Church and be in spiritual bondage, or leave the Church, and serve God in freedom of conscience?

He had to make the choice, but as soon as his mind was made up, he set his face towards Noyon. It was a long journey, but it was pleasant, for it was springtime – the spring of 1534. Arriving in his native town, he lingered in the old Cornmarket Square. He gazed at the house which had once been his home, and then went to the Cathedral, and stood before the Noyon clergy. He told them he had come to surrender the benefices which had been bestowed upon him in his youth. He said he could not be their priest. He had decided to leave the Church.

The men with their sober faces and their dark robes looked at him in astonishment. John was almost twenty-five, the accepted age for ordination to the priesthood. Some of these men had known him as a child. They had followed his career with interest, and had marvelled at his University successes. They had anticipated high honours coming to him in the Church. Now he was throwing away all his opportunities, and worst of all, he would be joining the detested Protestants!

What could these experienced churchmen say?

In bitterness and anger they dismissed him from their presence –

'Traitor, and wrecker of our Church, Go!'

John left the Cathedral sad at heart, yet feeling sure he had done God's will. Popular opinion in Noyon immediately judged him to be a 'heretic', and soon the authorities were looking for an opportunity to arrest him. It came when, on a certain occasion, a commotion occurred during a church service at which John was present.

The result of this episode was that John Calvin was imprisoned at Noyon on May 26th, 'for uproar made in the church on the eve of Holy Trinity.' He was consigned to the prison known as La Porte Corbaut. It was a small, strong building, with a courtroom, two cells, and two dark dungeons, well bolted and barred. Fortunately, he was kept there for a short time only. On his release, he took the road to Paris, knowing full well that there were new perils to be faced. He knew also that he could never return to Noyon. He had walked its streets for the last time.

IV
THEY MET IN SECRET

It was not safe for John to remain in France. He was a marked man. But he loved his country. How could he bring himself to leave his native land – perhaps for ever?

For a while he lived in Paris in disguise. Soon, however, the news of his conversion reached the little groups of believers. They heard that he was a new man, full of love for Christ and his gospel. Cautiously, they invited him to their secret meeting places, and gave him their secret pass-words. He felt that he himself needed to be taught, but they begged him to read from the life-giving Book – the Bible – and explain its deeper meaning. He was welcomed into the homes of the poor, and these people were encouraged and strengthened in their faith, as he spoke to them.

John, who had so loved the company of great men of learning, was now willing and eager to go anywhere for Christ.

Inevitably, the police got to know that he was in the capital, but he slipped away unnoticed, and found a home with friends at Poitiers. Again he preached to people gathered for worship deep in the woods. In a cave dimly lit by burning torches, he celebrated the Lord's Supper. There was no magnificent altar, with beautifully embroidered

Calvin 'welcomed into the homes of the poor'

altar-cloth and silver plate, and chalice. A flat rock served as the Table of the Lord, and the bread and wine were set forth in simplest fashion. But God was in that place.

Another necessary move took John once more to du Tillet's home, and thence on to Orleans. It was about this time – October, 1534, – that something very mysterious happened.

Early on the morning of the 18th, the citizens of Paris stepped out into the streets to find that large placards had been posted on walls and railings and public buildings. One poster even appeared on the door of the king's bedchamber at the castle of Amboise. Written in French, these notices were a violent and irreverent attack on the Roman Catholic Mass. The authorities became mad with rage, and the king himself was determined to take revenge. It was discovered that bundles of these placards had been smuggled into the country from abroad, but who had done the bill-posting? No one knew.

Every Protestant was a suspect. Hundreds of innocent people were arrested, and many were tortured and put to death. With such fierce persecution going on, Calvin knew he must seek refuge outside his own country – he must delay no longer. He contacted his friend, du Tillet, and together they set out on horseback for the German border and the Rhineland.

THE MAN OF GENEVA

The roads were bad, and the weather was bitterly cold. The inns were full, for travellers were anxious to complete their journeys before winter finally set in. At one stopping-place their money was stolen during the night, and they were left in sore straits. They dare not lodge a complaint, for the king's spies were everywhere, and they must not call attention to themselves. Fortunately a loyal servant who accompanied them had some money of his own. This he made available to his masters, and it was sufficient to meet their immediate expenses.

At another place they found themselves in rowdy company. Men were raising their tankards and toasting 'Old Harry' – Henry VIII, who had made himself head of the Church in England. It was their way of protesting against the heavy taxes demanded by Rome. The innkeeper looked round apprehensively. He was on tenterhooks, and quickly called for order, and a lively song, to take their minds off religion and politics.

At last, after a journey of over 200 miles, Calvin and du Tillet reached the safety of Strasbourg. Here there were Protestant pastors already busily engaged in helping French refugees. John, however, was anxious to settle in Basle, this being one of the chief centres of learning in Europe, and noted for its printers and printing presses.

Being keen to get on with his writing, John

reached Basle early in 1535, and rented a room in the suburbs. He was preparing a manual for Protestant believers. His aim was to set out in orderly manner the great doctrines of Scripture. Very few people in Basle knew who the newcomer was, for he called himself Martinus Lucanius.

One inhabitant of the city who was aware of the stranger's identity was Nicholas Cop, and it was natural that the two friends should meet. In fact Nicholas had been eagerly awaiting John's arrival. What discussions they had, night after night! First they talked of the goings-on in Paris, and John concluded:

'Francis has become more fickle, and he will no longer listen to the pleadings of his sister Marguerite. He seems to live only for his hunting and his banquets, his wine and his court ladies. The country is in a bad state.'

'It seems that things in England are not much better,' Nicholas commented.

'Well,' added John, 'I understand that, over there, the gospel is spreading.'

'True,' Nicholas replied, 'but spiritual reform and political craftiness do not work well together. Henry VIII wants power, absolute power, and a Church that will obey him. He despises the men of real faith in his land.'

John expressed some surprise, but Nicholas went on –

'Henry is prepared to banish or kill friend or foe, Protestant or Catholic, as it suits his purpose. Indeed, some of his subjects are seeking refuge over here. I was speaking the other day to a rich merchant who has business interests in England. He told me that the warehouses overlooking the Thames often afford temporary shelter to believers seeking freedom of worship.'

There was a pause in the conversation, but John wanted to hear more, so Nicholas filled in the details:

'You see, John, it works like this: In return for a considerable sum of money, a friendly merchant will agree to hide a wanted man in one of his warehouse attics. At dead of night the fugitive will creep stealthily to a side door and give a number of gentle knocks. A trusted night-watchman, fully briefed, will challenge the caller, who then will speak a secret name as password. The door will be opened, and he will be led, in utter darkness, up and down ladders, through trapdoors into storerooms filled with merchandise, along dark passages and up more steps. When the attic room is reached, his guide will leave him, and he will have to grope around to find the bed. The small window will be darkened, but even in the gloom the man's heart will be full of hope. Food and drink will be provided, and a bucket of clean water to wash in.

'That man may be confined in the attic for days, or even weeks, but when the ship sails for Antwerp he will be taken on board, hidden by the massive bales of wool being shipped to the Continent. Once he gets to Antwerp, he can make his way to a place of safety.'

'Most interesting!' John declared. For myself, I am content at the moment to be in Basle. I am unknown here, and my lodging at Madame Catherine Klein's is suitable for my purpose. I have quietness, and can concentrate on my writing.'

'You are working on a new book?' queried Nicholas. 'Tell me all about it.'

'Well, it is a kind of study-guide to the Bible, – a handbook for the people of the Reformation,' said John.

'Is it really necessary?' interrupted Nicholas.

'I believe it is vital,' his friend replied. 'The Roman Church has an elaborate system of theology. If we expect people to abandon this, we must give them something to take its place.'

'We have given them the Bible,' Nicholas reminded him.

'Yes, but God calls us to teach the truths of the Bible,' John insisted. 'My plan is to explain the great doctrines which have been summarized in the Apostles' Creed, so that our people can understand the true meaning of the Holy Scriptures.

THE MAN OF GENEVA

I am writing about the passages in the Bible which show that it is Christ alone, and not the Church, or the priests, or the mass, but Christ only, who is the Saviour of sinners. Then, I plan to write about the way in which the Holy Spirit helps us to live the Christian life, and also what the sacraments of Baptism and the Lord's Supper really mean.

'When I have written my book I will dedicate it to King Francis, and in my dedicatory letter I shall defend the faith of the Protestants. I will plead the cause of the godly, indeed the cause of Christ himself.'

'Do you really think, John, that Francis will read your letter or your book?', Nicholas enquired.

'I do not know. I hope he will. At least I shall feel that I have done my duty,' John said, a little impatiently. There was a moment's silence; then he continued thoughtfully: 'The printing presses are helping the Reformation. I know that the majority of the population can neither read nor write, but when they see books in print, they will want to learn.'

At this point, Nicholas broke in excitedly:

'I am reminded, John, of something else my friend the merchant, told me. He said that in England he was acquainted with some ladies of noble birth who had responded to the New Learning. Now they are holding classes for their chief servants, and teaching them to read the Bible. Do you not think that this is wonderful?'

'Yes, I do,' replied John, 'but now I must be going, for I have a great deal to do. Thank you for all you have told me.'

*

A few months later, John took his manuscript to a shop which carried the sign of the Black Bear, for here lived his friend Thomas Platter, the printer. In March, 1536, *The Institutes of the Christian Religion*, that is, 'Instruction in Christianity', was on sale at the bookstalls. Its title page, in Latin, named the author as John Calvin of Noyon. Its Preface was addressed to King Francis I of France, to whom Calvin offered his book as a confession of faith.

But when men looked for the author, he could not be found. Madame Klein's lodger had left Basle for an unknown destination.

V
ADVENTURES IN ITALY

The two travellers crossing the Alps into Italy were very tired, yet they knew they must still press on. Indeed, their goal was almost in sight. They were going to the great castle of Duke Hercules of Ferrara. But how would they be received? That was the question which made them feel uneasy. They were sure that the Duchess Renée, a Princess of France, would give them a warm welcome, for it was at her invitation that the journey had been undertaken. But what of the Duke? He was an ardent Roman Catholic, being indeed the grandson of a Pope. Church officials continually were urging him to weed out the Protestants in his territory.

Calvin and his friend du Tillet were discussing these matters when the walls of Ferrara came into view.

'Perhaps he will be away on some military expedition,' du Tillet hopefully suggested.

'I don't think so. That would be too good to be true, but remember it is the Duchess whom we want to see.'

At the court the two men would be known as Charles d'Espeville and Louis de Hautmont. Fortunately the Duchess had a secretary – Clement Marot by name – who favoured the Reformation.

He was able to ensure that the Frenchmen were given a courteous admittance when they presented themselves at the castle gates.

The Duchess of Ferrara was a truly remarkable woman. She was the daughter of King Louis XII of France, and would have been heir to the throne if the law of the land had permitted a woman to become its Queen. From her early years she took an intelligent interest in all that was going on, and from the old professor Lefèvre, and from her cousin Marguerite, she had learned about the new faith, and was attracted to it.

Renée's marriage to the Italian duke had not been of her choosing, but had been arranged for political reasons, as so often was the custom in those days.

Intensely fond of her native country, the young princess felt like an exile in Italy, and it was natural that she should determine to do everything in her power to help her own people. French refugees, especially those who professed the Protestant faith, found a place at her court, and men of learning were drawn into the inner circle of her friendship. At first, her husband did not oppose this, but pressure from Rome gradually destroyed his tolerance.

Calvin and du Tillet were conducted to their rooms, and were glad to rest and refresh themselves before assembling with the courtiers and royal ladies and many distinguished guests. It was a well-established tradition that life at the court should be gay, with a continual round of balls and banquets. John would have preferred something more serious, but he performed his part well, and many admired the handsome young Frenchman with his charming manners and entertaining conversation.

After a few days, however, the newly-arrived visitors became aware that they were being eyed suspiciously by Catholic dignitaries at the court, and John immediately realized that their stay must not be prolonged. His intention of having lengthy discussions on the Bible with men of similar views to his own would have to be modified. He would hope, however, that a long talk with the Duchess on spiritual themes would still be possible.

In a little private chapel adjoining his room, the conversation took place. John seemed to have a foreboding that dark and terrible days lay ahead for Renée. He begged her to keep true to her faith in Christ. He told her of his new book, *The Institutes*, and his hopes for the future of the Reformation. He promised to pray for her.

By arrangement with Marot the secretary, Calvin and du Tillet quietly left the castle one morning at daybreak, and rode on again towards the Alps. The return to Basle was fairly leisurely, as John wanted to do some missionary work in the towns and villages. By deciding in favour of the route that included the St. Bernard Pass, the pilgrims could make a brief stay at Aosta, and see for themselves the religious situation in the Alpine valley.

Du Tillet was less enthusiastic than on earlier expeditions. John noticed it, and wondered if his friend would go back to the Roman Church. Outwardly, du Tillet had never left the Church. Indeed, this was the position of a number of leading men at this time. They preached and taught the Protestant faith, and often suffered for their beliefs, but had never completely severed their allegiance to Rome. This caused Calvin great unhappiness and concern. Indeed, while he was at Ferrara he wrote some important letters, including one to a former friend, Gérard Roussel, who had been a disciple of Lefèvre, a spiritual adviser to Marguerite of Navarre, and a foremost preacher of the reformed faith.

Quite recently, Roussel had been appointed Bishop of Oloron, and this had aroused Calvin's indignation. So his letter began:

'John Calvin, to a former friend, now a Prelate . . . ' He accused Roussel of deserting the cause, and going over to the enemy. It was clear that John regarded Roussel as a traitor. It was equally clear to those who were watching the events, that John Calvin was becoming more militant.

*

Arriving at Basle in safety, Calvin and du Tillet separated, for John wanted to pay yet another visit to Paris. This was possible because King Francis had modified his policy in dealing with French 'heretics.' He issued an Edict which permitted any person charged with heresy to return from exile. Such a person would have six months' grace in which to consider his ways. He then would be required to return to the Catholic fold. It was no change of heart which moved the king. Rather, it was a compromise, in an endeavour to win the favour of the German Protestants, who had been offended by the king's brutal methods of suppression in the affair of the Placards of 1534. Francis was involved in a new war with Charles V, and he desperately needed the help of the German princes and their peoples.

John Calvin's motive for going to Paris was strictly personal. He had a few business matters to attend to, but in particular, he wished to arrange for his younger brother Antoine, who was in Paris, and his sister Marie, to follow him abroad. They had become Protestants.

The city had lost its attraction for John, and his stay there was brief. Many of his dear friends had suffered martyrdom. He could visit their homes no more, and he felt very sad. Therefore he left, as suddenly and silently as he had arrived. His intention was to go to Strasbourg, but the most direct route was blocked because of the war. Troops with military equipment of all kinds were in transit, and he was obliged to choose a roundabout journey through Geneva. He reached this city on a summer evening, travel-stained and hungry. Answering the challenge of the armed sentry at the Cornavin Gate, he was given a certificate with which he would gain admittance and lodging at one of the inns. He crossed the drawbridge and was soon on the lookout for a suitable lodging-place.

Once at the inn, a good meal and some rest quickly restored his flagging spirits. He planned to go to bed early, and continue his travels the next morning. That very night, however, an unexpected visitor called, and asked permission to see John Calvin. The landlord knocked and entered John's room.

'Master William Farel waits to speak to you, Sir. He says his message is urgent.'

'Ask him to come in,' John replied, and almost immediately a stocky, red-bearded, fearless-looking Frenchman stood in the doorway. John guessed he would be between forty-five and fifty years of age.

Farel preaching in the open-air

THE MAN OF GENEVA

As a youth, Farel had left his home at Gap in Dauphiné to go to college in Paris. He became a student and disciple of Lefèvre. Responding to the Bible message, he was filled with a burning zeal to preach the gospel everywhere.

'God will renovate the world, and you will live to see it,' the old professor had told him.

Thus William Farel became an ardent reformer. His methods were far from gentle. He was like some John the Baptist calling the people to repent and turn to the Lord. He was extremely antagonistic to the Roman Church, and all its practices.

John's hopes for a quiet night were shattered. As he rose from his chair to greet the visitor, he felt a strange uneasiness coming over him.

'What brings you here, Master Farel?', he demanded.

'I come in the name of the Lord,' said Farel boldly. 'I was told you had entered Geneva, and could be found at this lodging-place. My message is, that you must stay in this city, and help in the work of reform. The old order has gone for ever, and you must build up the new.'

'Calvin! this is a matter of the utmost importance. A year ago, the religion of Rome ceased to be the recognized religion of Geneva, and I am sure you will have heard the latest news. It is wonderful, praise be to God! On Sunday, the 21st

THE MAN OF GENEVA

May, in this year of our Lord, 1536, the people of Geneva, by command of the city councils, gathered at St. Pierre's. As bell and trumpet sounded forth, they crowded into the Cathedral, led by the chief magistrate. Lifting their right hands to heaven they solemnly declared their full acceptance of the Protestant faith.

'Do you not know, Master Calvin, that the monasteries and convents have been closed, the Mass is forbidden, and monks and nuns and priests are quickly leaving the city? The nunnery of St. Claire has been turned into a hospital, and a monastery has become a school for the children of the poor. Geneva's territory includes twenty-eight villages, and preachers are being sent to establish the new worship.

'Calvin, you are needed – you must stay!'

John raised his hand to interrupt the torrent of words.

'No! No! that work is not for me. I am a scholar, and my work is to write books. I cannot do what you ask.'

'But you *must*,' stormed Farel.

As the argument went on and on, John, pale and frightened, begged his visitor to leave him in peace, but Farel would not go. At last, the older man rose to his feet, and his manner was threatening.

'You, John Calvin, insist on the importance of

your studies, but I declare in the name of Almighty God, that his curse will come upon you if you refuse your help in this work, for then you will be seeking your own interests, instead of the honour of Christ.'

Farel stopped speaking, and a deathly hush filled the room. John bowed his head. He was no longer conscious of Farel's presence.

'It seemed as if God from heaven had laid his mighty hand upon me, to arrest me,' he said afterwards.

The battle was over. John Calvin would obey God's will by remaining in Geneva, and Farel was satisfied. From that hour, the older man served the younger. In this lay Farel's greatness. He himself had done a good work in Geneva, but Calvin could do more. He recognized Calvin's mastermind, and for the rest of his life he was John's devoted disciple and servant, colleague and friend.

VI
THE CITY ON THE LAKE

The next morning, though still rather dazed by his encounter with Farel, John decided to take a walk, and explore the city which was to become his home.

Geneva was built on the rock beside the blue waters of Lake Léman, and was encircled by mountains, with the majestic, snow-capped Mont Blanc towering above the other peaks. John felt a deep sense of awe as he gazed upon the scene, but he reminded himself that he was not in Geneva as a tourist. Soon he was walking up the steep little street which led to the Cathedral of St. Pierre. Entering the great stone building, he was struck with its bareness, for it had been stripped of its images and altars.

Yes, the Reformation had come to Geneva, but John was not happy as he returned to the inn. Certainly he was impressed by the prosperity which had come to the city through its skilled craftsmen and its merchants. He was glad that it was a busy, thriving place, a centre of trade where the products of France, Germany and Italy were marketed. It was the worldliness of the inhabitants which distressed him. When the day's work was done, the taverns were filled. Drunken men stumbled through the streets. Gambling with dice and cards went on, hour after hour. The ladies wore eye-catching gowns, richly adorned with jewels, while men of wealth and leisure strutted about in fine clothes.

The citizens, led by their Councils, had indeed voted for Protestantism, but Calvin knew that Geneva was not the ideal city of God. The legal constitution could not change men's hearts and create a living Church.

Looking back on Geneva's long history – a sad and complicated story of war and bloodshed – John remembered that he was but a small boy when the Protestant faith first took root in Switzerland. At the centre of the movement was Ulrich Zwingli, a man who in early life had been a gay young priest, but turning to the Bible had found salvation and peace through faith in the Lord Jesus Christ. Zwingli soon became a mighty man of God, a gifted preacher and a clear-sighted theologian. He was killed at Kappel in 1531, in a battle between Protestant Zurich and the Catholic cantons or states. He had gone out, a zealous soldier of the Cross, accompanying the army as a chaplain rather than as a fighter. He met his death while ministering to the wounded.

Reflecting on these events of the past, suddenly John's mind switched to the happenings of the night before, and he shuddered! Again he saw in

Geneva (17th century)

his mind's eye William Farel, with arm upraised, standing over him, fierce, fiery and threatening. Yes, it was William Farel – very much alive – with whom he had to deal. They must have a long, calm talk together about the work of God.

John knew that Farel was dedicated to the work in Geneva. In 1532, the missionary-minded powerful canton of Bern had sent him there to evangelize the French-speaking peoples of the city.

Farel was mobbed by hostile crowds, set upon by angry priests and their agents, knocked and struck in the face by gangs of hooligans, but he did not give in. With the help of two companions he continued to preach and to teach, and eventually the Genevan authorities sent soldiers to protect the missionaries.

'In truth, Farel is a great man and for the gospel's sake I ought to be proud to work with him', John told himself, as he paused to open the door of the inn parlour, and join the other travellers.

*

It was necessary for Calvin to return to Basle to collect his belongings, but he was soon back in Geneva, and was given the appointment of 'Professor of Sacred Letters in the Church of Geneva.' It was a high-sounding title, but, due to an over-

THE MAN OF GENEVA

sight, for the first five months he received no payment for his work. There was slackness also on the part of the secretary who recorded the Council Minutes, for John was described without name, simply as 'that Frenchman.'

Clearly nobody expected that Calvin would make any great impact, and at first only a small group of people gathered in St. Pierre's to hear his lectures on the Epistles of Paul. To make matters worse, he was far from well, and he found it quite a strain climbing the steep slope to the cathedral entrance, and then exerting himself to speak for an hour each day in that great building.

Of all John's friends, only William Farel seemed to be really optimistic about the future. John could not help noticing how popular Farel was with the people. They admired his courage, his forthright methods when defending the gospel, and the way he stood up to his enemies. All this seemed to place Calvin at a disadvantage, but he had given his word to Farel and he must stay. He felt like a sentry at the post of duty – he was under Divine Orders.

Within a few weeks an unexpected opportunity came John's way. A Public Debate was scheduled to take place at nearby Lausanne, the chief city of canton Vaud. The point in history had been reached where each canton was at liberty to choose its own religion, and Lausanne wished to settle the question as to whether or not it should adopt the Protestant faith.

Farel was to take a leading part, and his first engagement would be to preach the Sunday sermon. Then, at 7 o'clock precisely on the Monday morning, the important discussions would begin. It was a great responsibility, and Farel felt he needed Calvin's support, so the two men set out together. Knowing that the inns would become crowded with delegates, they arrived early, and so were nicely settled before the invasion of visitors began.

On the Saturday evening, there was time for John to have a look round the city. Without his academic robes he appeared younger than his twenty-seven years, and as he mingled with the crowds, more than one bystander took a second glance at him. He was careful about his personal appearance, and his stylish dark clothes were enhanced by a pure white pleated front and ruff. He carried a pair of embroidered gloves, and wore a large ring on his left hand. His soft flat hat was slightly tilted. It was, however, his fine intelligent face which attracted attention. The dark, penetrating eyes which were always alert, the expression of understanding and sympathy, and the smile which lit up the well-defined features, portrayed a man of character. The curly forked

THE MAN OF GENEVA

beard which was well-combed, seemed to give an added dignity.

John found it interesting to listen to speakers holding forth in the city square, and to hear the more homely but animated conversations of friends and relatives meeting after long absences. He noted the banners of the opposing religious groups, with their striking mottoes. When he returned to the inn and went to bed at a late hour, he was full of eagerness for the great debate.

The programme went forward as planned, and the sessions lasted for eight days. More than three hundred priests had been invited, but less than two-thirds of that number turned up. The Protestants attended in full force. To make sure that everything was done fairly, Bern sent five deputies, resplendent in their broad-brimmed feathered hats, their black doublets and their bright red hose. Serious-looking secretaries with their parchments, their ink-horns and their quill pens, waited to write down all the proceedings.

Farel had prepared ten theses for discussion. Another important figure was Pierre Viret, a highly respected pastor in Lausanne. Though he was ready for anything, Calvin regarded himself as an observer rather than a speaker.

Long before the appointed hour, the Cathedral was filled to overflowing. Day after day people packed the building, and crowds stood outside.

Everyone wanted to get a good view of the contestants, and necks were craned uncomfortably. To the astonishment of the audience, only four priests as members of the Catholic party stood up to address the assembly, and they were ill-equipped for the task, their arguments being, in the main unconvincing. Yet one speaker for Rome did manage clearly to state the Roman Catholic doctrine of the Eucharist, and quoted the Church Fathers as his authority. 'You have ignored the teaching of the Fathers, and you stand condemned,' he told the Protestant delegates.

At this, Calvin could keep silent no longer. He signalled his desire to take part, and rose to address the great gathering.

Calvin was well acquainted with the writings of the early Christian thinkers and leaders. It had been part of his training at the Collège de Montaigu in Paris. Again, the Sacrament of the Lord's Supper, which was being debated, was a subject he regarded as vital and sacred. To discover its true meaning and significance, he had spent many hours in diligent study since his conversion.

A great gulf was fixed between the doctrine held by his opponents and Calvin's simple but profound belief that the Lord is truly present in the Sacrament. But he denied the Roman teaching that the bread and wine were actually *changed* into the body and blood of Jesus.

John Calvin spoke as a man inspired. Without notes, but with great skill, he quoted accurately from Chrysostom, Augustine and many others, and in doing so, he inserted the vital phrases which the priest had omitted. Then he quoted freely from the Holy Scriptures, and the priest had no answer.

There was a stir in the audience, for people were deeply moved. A Franciscan monk cried out in an agony of conviction:

'God have mercy upon me! God forgive me! Calvin's teaching is the true doctrine. I have followed Rome for too long.'

The vast assembly was gripped! Some were startled, some fell to their knees in prayer, and some wept. The Debate ran its appointed course, but the outcome was never in doubt. Lausanne and its surrounding territories became officially Protestant, and there was tremendous rejoicing.

The news spread quickly, and as a result, Calvin's name no longer was unknown. From Lausanne he went to Bern, and then back to Geneva.

VII
CONTENDING WITH THE COUNCILS

In a house not far from the Cathedral of St. Pierre a man sat at a table writing. Again and again he dipped his quill into the inkhorn, and the parchment pages became filled with words. Calvin and Farel had decided that the Church in Geneva must have a set of rules! As, however, the Church was tied to the State, these rules would have to be approved by the City councils, before they could be put into operation. In many ways the most important of Geneva's governing bodies was the Little Council, consisting of four Syndics, or chief magistrates, a Treasurer, and twenty others, making a total of twenty-five members. Then came the Council of the Two Hundred, and the Council of the Sixty, each having its own special function. In matters of exceptional importance, a General Assembly could be summoned. This larger council was comprised of all the heads of households in the city.

At first the demands of Farel and Calvin were viewed with favour, but not for long. When the reformers produced not only a confession of Faith and a Catechism, but a four-point Plan entitled 'Articles for the Ruling of the Church', they quickly ran into trouble.

View in the Alps

The Articles dealt with:

(1) The Celebration of The Lord's Supper.
(2) The Singing of Psalms.
(3) The Religious Instruction of Children.
(4) Marriage.

It was Article one which caused the controversy. Calvin and Farel claimed that they should have the authority to debar from the Lord's Table any person holding false doctrine, and any person whose life was immoral. Such persons they claimed, should first be urged to repent, but if they remained stubborn and unwilling to receive correction, then they should be excommunicated.

*

Uproar broke out in the Council Chamber of Geneva's Town Hall as the Right Honourable Gentlemen of the Little Council debated the document which had been drafted and presented by 'those foreigners'.

'Do you see that word?' shouted one councillor. "Excommunication!" The preachers want us to give them the power to turn people away from the Lord's Table. They call it discipline, but who are they, to judge others?'

'Calvin wants to set himself up as the new Pope, a Protestant Pope,' said another.

'We have got rid of one kind of slavery, only

to find ourselves threatened by a worse kind,' a third member exclaimed.

Above the din, yet another voice was heard —

'Gentlemen! I heard him myself. This man Calvin denounced us, the City Fathers, as a "council of the devil"'.

'Shame! Shame!' they cried in chorus. 'We will not allow this foreigner to tell the people of Geneva how to behave.'

When the clamour and heat of argument had subsided, there were some who spoke up for Calvin and Farel. There were many good things, they said, in the Four-point Plan. At last the conclusion was reached that Articles Two, Three and Four could be accepted, but Article One must be amended — the Council alone had the authority to excommunicate, and the pastors could not be granted that power.

The Catechism presented no problems, and the Confession of Faith would be binding on all citizens. While in May, 1536, the crowds had flocked to St. Pierre's formally to declare their acceptance of the Protestant faith, now a more personal affirmation would be required. So, in groups of ten, the population was ordered to gather in the Cathedral to take the oath of allegiance.

Soon the reformers discovered that some inhabitants were refusing to obey these new regulations. It was clear that many people had turned to Protestantism for reasons other than love to the Lord Jesus Christ.

No wonder that John felt defeated and miserable.

'Why ever did I come here?' he asked again and again. 'But I must ride out the storm,' he told Farel. But even as he spoke, more storm-clouds were gathering.

Two Anabaptist missionaries arrived in Geneva. They came from the Netherlands, and belonged to a Protestant group which was spreading rapidly. They acquired their name because they held the view that baptism was for true believers only, as a witness to their faith in Christ, and not for infants who were too young to understand. As they refused to accept infant baptism they required Christians to be baptized again. Hence the name *Ana* baptist, meaning 'baptized again'. These people also believed that the Christian community should be completely independent, and separate from the State. Most of the Anabaptists were good, peaceable folk who wanted to follow literally the New Testament pattern. Some of their leaders, however, were extremely fanatical, with the result that in every city they visited, they were viewed with suspicion by the civic powers.

What the two Dutch Anabaptists wanted was a Public Debate with the Genevan preachers, so they approached the Council for the necessary permission. Reluctantly the licence was granted chiefly because of Farel's insistence.

Under the watchful eyes of Council members the Debate went on for two long days. Calvin and Farel were against the new missionaries, but it was obvious that the citizens listened eagerly, and occasionally applauded the Dutchmen. This annoyed the authorities who were afraid of public disturbance and breaches of the peace. Therefore, swift action was taken. The Council of the Two Hundred seized the papers of the opposing parties, and ordered the Debate to stop. They then declared that the Anabaptists had lost the contest. The Dutchmen, on pain of death, were banished from the city.

The decision did not please everyone, and there were murmurings as the audience filed out of the building.

'Those Dutchmen spoke well,' said one man to his neighbour.

'I agree with you,' his friend replied, 'and did you notice that Calvin lost his temper, and Farel, as usual, was most aggressive?'

'Yes, I saw it, but I think Master Calvin is in poor health these days.' The speaker would have continued, but a nudge from someone's elbow caused him to look round. Then he knew it was a warning to be quiet, for a short distance away stood one of the magistrates, very stern and sullen.

Another storm arose when a certain Pastor in Lausanne named Caroli, who had a grudge against Calvin, brought a charge against the Genevan reformers, the serious charge of teaching false doctrine. The man had been scrutinizing the 'Articles for the Ruling of the Church,' and imagined he saw a weak spot. There was no mention of the Holy Trinity.

Calvin and Farel were furious! Of course they believed that Jesus is God – believed it strongly. For Caroli to insinuate that they did *not* believe in the Trinity was outrageous. They hurried to Lausanne to defend themselves, before a special Synod. In the end, Calvin won his case, but he and his colleague were very upset by the experience.

There was more trouble ahead! Calvin's friend du Tillet had been in Geneva for some time, and was unhappy about the religious situation. Once, everything seemed favourable to the Protestant cause in Geneva; now, all was chaos. He was a man who disliked the sound of battle, whether military, political or religious. Ever since his visit to Italy as John's travelling companion, he had been pondering the question, 'Which way shall I take?' He was a man of mild disposition, and would have preferred a kind of semi-Protestantism which would give credence to the New Learning, while retaining its links with the past.

Calvin and Farel were so forthright and uncompromising that Louis du Tillet wondered where it would all end.

As soon as du Tillet had made up his mind, he left Geneva secretly, without saying 'Farewell' to his friends. Later, Calvin received a letter, and when he had broken the seal, he read:

'Is it not the case, that all these troubles have come upon you as God's correction to recall you to the true Church?'

The words cut deeply into Calvin's heart. He read on. Yes, it was as he had feared – du Tillet was returning to the Catholic Church.

Thus John lost a friend who had meant so much to him in earlier years. He felt abandoned and very lonely.

Convinced of their mission, however, the Reformers were determined to press forward whatever the cost, but their difficulties were increased when in the Elections of February, 1538, the Little Council suffered a complete political overturn. The new Syndics were men opposed to Calvin and Farel, and it was not long before relations between Church and State became strained. If only Calvin and his colleagues had been a little more moderate in their demands, and more gentle in their approach, they might still have won success. Unfortunately, they did not take kindly to criticism, even when it came from friends.

CONTENDING WITH THE COUNCILS

A certain Thomas Grynaeus at Basle wrote a letter to Calvin and Farel urging them to be moderate, and reminding them that no man is infallible. It had no effect.

In March, the crisis came to a head, when the Councils decided to follow the Bernese pattern in Church worship. Bern had stressed the need to have uniformity in the churches of southern Switzerland. So Geneva's government issued orders which directly affected Calvin and his associates in the ministry. In particular, unleavened bread was to be used in the Lord's Supper, the font was to be used in the Baptismal service, the festivals of Christmas, Easter, Ascension and Pentecost were to be observed, and a bride could be adorned in festive array on her wedding day. Farel had abolished these practices in the Genevan Church, in his zeal to eliminate all that savoured of Rome. Now they would be re-introduced.

Calvin himself was not strongly opposed to these things, but he was greatly annoyed, as were all the pastors, that the city councils had acted without first consulting the Reformers. It seemed that the Little Council was bent on diminishing Calvin's authority, and it was evident that if the Reformers administered the Church discipline which they deemed necessary, then they would be accused of defying the government.

*

THE MAN OF GENEVA

In the city lived a faithful pastor named Coraud, a man almost blind and in poor health, but one who had loyally assisted Calvin and Farel in the work of the Lord. He had the audacity to get up in the pulpit and denounce the Council members as 'drunkards,' and 'rats among the straw.' He was seized and taken to prison. Hearing this, his friends went to the Town Hall and demanded his release.

As Calvin and Farel themselves were in disgrace because of their refusal to give a definite answer about the Bernese 'ceremonies', they were not received very favourably. Bitter words were spoken, and the two men had reason to fear for their own safety.

Outside, a mob gathered, waving clubs and shouting that the preachers should be flung into the Rhone, and left to drown. As Calvin and Farel left the Council Chamber they wondered whether they would ever get through the seething mass of people. They were hissed and spat upon. As Calvin doggedly pushed his way towards home, with Farel close behind, he repeatedly heard the derisive word 'Cain, Cain', shouted after him.

The following day was Easter Day, and a friend brought news that the Councils were holding emergency meetings. As nightfall brought darkness, the sound of musket-fire was heard outside John's house, and angry men swarmed around the shuttered window and heavily-bolted door. Then a new call sounded out –

'Make way for the herald! Make way for the herald. Geneva's Council commands you – Make way!'

The crowd divided and became silent. A man in herald's uniform, and carrying a silver-topped cane, stopped at Calvin's door. His attendants held their lanterns high, and with loud rap-tapping demanded that the Council's messenger be granted admittance. Once inside, the official proceeded to read the ultimatum.

Briefly, Calvin was informed that he and Farel must administer the sacrament on Easter Day according to the Bernese regulations.

'If you refuse to do so,' the messenger said, 'then, by order of the Syndics, you are forbidden to preach.' The Council required a clear 'Yes' or 'No'. But Farel was not at home, and Calvin would make no promise.

The herald had performed his duty. He left the house, and the crowd in the street resumed its abusive threatenings against the pastors.

VIII
BANISHED FROM GENEVA

April 21st dawned fair and bright. People were out early, for it was Easter morning. Rumours had been spreading, and there was great excitement. St. Pierre's was overflowing long before the appointed hour of service, and the church of St. Gervais across the river, was also packed. But there was no atmosphere of reverence or spirit of worship. Instead, there was speculation as to whether or not the pastors would occupy their pulpits. Easter Day was very special in the Church Calendar, and the congregations expected to receive the sacrament.

When Calvin mounted the pulpit steps, he confronted a people whose faces clearly showed how angry and hostile they were. He told them plainly that there could be no celebration of the Lord's Supper in such circumstances of popular tumult. They were sinning against the Lord by their riotous behaviour. But no disturbance took place.

Meanwhile, in the pulpit of St. Gervais, Farel was making a similar announcement, but without the calmness which was so typical of his friend. Such was the response that his supporters had to intervene to protect him from the threats of his enemies. For Calvin, however, worse was to follow at the evening service held in the Church of Rive, beside the shores of Lake Geneva. As he entered the building it was already packed full. In recent days men had been running amock past his house, shouting and yelling, 'To the Rhone! To the Rhone!' They had fired their primitive guns outside his windows, sometimes fifty or sixty times. He was in no doubt what *they* wanted to do to *him*! Now these same men were sitting in his congregation, the handles of their swords reflecting the evening light. Before, he had heard their angry voices, but now he was looking into the very eyes of these sworn enemies. Did he remember the words of Jesus, 'Pray for them which despitefully use you?' Did he recall the promise of God, 'I will never leave you nor forsake you?' Did he wonder if this was to be his last sermon?

As he began to speak, the infuriated men rushed forward, menacingly waving their drawn swords at the preacher. His friends rushed forward to protect him. But Calvin simply stood his ground. He knew that a man is always safest when he is doing the will of God, and his calm dignity and authority won the day. Swords were once again sheathed, and, as one local magistrate later wrote, 'The affair passed off without bloodshed.' It was, as another observer described it, 'a sort of miracle.' But even so, Calvin's life was still in danger, and his friends gathered round him, to protect him,

Calvin threatened, a scene in the church at Rive in 1538

BANISHED FROM GENEVA

and escort him back to the comparative peace and quiet of his own home.

Nevertheless, Calvin and Farel had disobeyed the orders of the Council. They knew that it was an offence which could not be overlooked. Late on that Sunday night the Syndics met. On Easter Monday, the Council of Two Hundred gathered, and on the Tuesday, a meeting of the General Assembly was convened and sentence was passed.

Again the preachers had a visit from the Council's messenger. Calvin, Farel and Coraud (who had been released from jail), were ordered to leave the city within three days. They were banished from Geneva!

'Well indeed,' said Calvin, 'if we had served men we should have been ill-repaid, but we serve a great Master who will amply reward us.'

The three men gathered up their few belongings, and horses were hired from the hostelry. On the morning of their departure, they found the stable-boy in tattered clothes, slouching against the stable door. He was bad-tempered at being called to his duty at such an early hour.

'Masters, your horses are ready,' he muttered.

The beasts were ill-fed, tired-looking creatures, but the exiled men made no complaint. Coraud, frail and ill, was placed upon a dusky-coloured mare, Calvin rode a dapple-grey, and Farel a chestnut hack. A bunch of spectators jeered as they reached the draw-bridge. When they had crossed the moat and were out of the city, the pastors heaved a great sigh of relief. They had covered but a few miles when the weak and half-blind Coraud slumped over his horse's shaggy neck. John quickly dismounted, and gave the reins of his own beast to Farel. He unstrapped a flask in his saddle-bag, and held it to Coraud's lips, and the sick man was able to drink a little. Then John climbed up behind Coraud to support him, and taking the reins from his feeble hands, urged the horse forward with its double burden.

The going was slow. They halted at a town where the blind pastor was well-known, and left him in the care of reliable friends.

Calvin and Farel decided to proceed to Bern and give their own personal account of what had happened. When they had done this, they pushed on to Zurich, to testify before the Synod, which was due to assemble on April 28th.

The Protestant cantons were deeply concerned to maintain peace in their parishes, and even Bern, notwithstanding its love of uniformity in church worship, felt that the evangelists had been judged too harshly. Zurich, while expressing its concern that the pastors had been expelled, considered it necessary to admonish Calvin to show more tender-heartedness towards his congregations. A movement was set in motion at once to get the reformers reinstated. Letters passed to and fro, and a delegation from Bern went to Geneva to recommend that the rejected men be invited back, and restored to their former posts.

It was all in vain. Geneva stubbornly refused to allow Calvin and Farel to re-enter the city.

The two friends were faced with a problem. Where should they go? Which city would give them a welcome? Calvin's thoughts centred on Basle, and as the choice was acceptable to Farel, they turned their horses' heads in that direction, though the journey would be at least 125 miles.

Away from the area of tumult and strain, they had time and opportunity to reflect upon the events which had led to their banishment. John was overwhelmed with a great wave of regret.

'I have been too hasty; I have tried to accomplish too much in too short a time, and I have shown myself to be unskilled in the work of the Lord,' he confessed. Farel too, was ready to admit failure, so with heavy hearts they faced the unknown future.

It was Spring-time, yet the weather was cold and stormy. The rains had swollen the streams and rivers, and on one occasion, when attempting to wade through the flood, the two nearly lost their lives. Soaked to the skin, and utterly exhausted, they reached Basle at last, destitute and penniless. The church at Basle was very kind to them both. The chief pastor, Grynaeus, made provision for Calvin, and the printer, Oporin, gave hospitality to Farel. To be received so cordially cheered the spirits of the travellers.

*

The Reformation had reached the town of Neuchâtel through the efforts of William Farel in earlier years. Now he received an invitation to return, and take up his former work. Believing this to be the call of God, he accepted, and soon was established as minister of the Neuchâtel church.

Calvin wanted to stay in Basle, and do more writing. There were many points in the first edition of his *Institutes* which he hoped to develop. The peace and freedom from interruption which he needed, surely could be found there. Alas for his hopes of quiet seclusion!

'Come over and help us,' came the cry from Strasbourg.

'No,' replied Calvin, 'I cannot come.'

The call became more urgent. Martin Bucer and other important men pleaded with him to make Strasbourg his home. They reminded him of the many French refugees in the town. And they needed a pastor. Still, Calvin declined. The truth was, he was so grieved by his lack of success in

Geneva, that he was afraid to attempt similar work in Strasbourg lest that, too, should end in failure.

Fortunately, Bucer was a man of tenacity, and he and his friends continued to remonstrate with the reluctant reformer.

'You are running away from your duty. If you disobey God's call, the Almighty will seek you out as he sought out his rebellious servant Jonah. Then you will stand guilty before God.'

The warning made a powerful impression upon Calvin, and he took heed, just as he had done when Farel, two years earlier, had challenged him to work in Geneva.

So Calvin went to Strasbourg, and spent three surprisingly happy years there.

The Reformation had come to Strasbourg in 1523. It was introduced peacefully, and indeed, its prime mover, Matthias Zell, had declared:

'Whosoever recognizes Christ as his Master and Saviour shall have a place at my table, and I also shall have a place with him in heaven.'

Thus the Protestant position was rather less rigid than in some other cities which had adopted the reformed faith. Great statesmen, scholars and theologians had been attracted to Strasbourg, making it a centre of learning and culture.

Calvin discovered in Martin Bucer the qualities of wise and warm-hearted friendship which he specially needed at that time. Bucer was a man of wide experience, immense sympathy and deep understanding, but he could be firm when occasion demanded. He was a spiritual leader far above the average, and was regarded as second only to Luther and Melanchthon. And so with Bucer's encouragement Calvin began his new ministry in the Church of St. Nicholas near the south wall of the city. His congregation was eager and appreciative. These people facing death for their faith in their native France, had fled to Strasbourg on the German border, seeking freedom to worship God according to their conscience. To hear Calvin preach the gospel in French was a great joy.

For a time Calvin lived in Bucer's house. It was a most hospitable home, with Bucer's wife Elizabeth proving herself a gracious and charming hostess.

Martin Bucer was Pastor of St. Thomas' Church, not far from the magnificent Roman Catholic Cathedral, a Gothic masterpiece, and famous for its giant astronomical clock.

Gradually Calvin became adjusted to his new sphere. He was respected by spiritual and civic leaders alike. In 1539 he was enrolled in the Guild of Tailors, and was made a citizen of Strasbourg. It was necessary to be a member of a Trade Guild, in order to obtain the privilege of citizenship. But his greatest pleasure was to minister to the needs of his flock. He held frequent services in his church on week-days as well as Sundays. The Lord's Supper was observed monthly. He was able to introduce the Church discipline which he believed was essential for the spiritual prosperity of the congregation. However, he did not go as far as an actual excommunication!

Calvin was delighted to find that his community of French refugees loved singing, and he prepared a hymn-book for use in public worship. It contained a small selection of Psalms, translated and set to music.

During his three years in the city, Calvin wrote some of his finest expositions, including his famous Commentary on Romans, and his teaching and preaching ministry extended far beyond the limits of his own congregation. John Sturm had just opened his new High School, and Calvin was appointed Lecturer in Holy Scripture. More and more opportunities came his way, yet Calvin was desperately poor. Du Tillet wrote, generously offering money, but as that gentleman had returned to the Roman Church, Calvin felt that he could not accept it.

After a while, John left Bucer's pleasant home to rent a house and take students as boarders, though financially this was not of much benefit.

A heavier cross was placed upon Calvin when

the trouble-maker Caroli turned up in Strasbourg and endeavoured to belittle the French pastor in the eyes of Martin Bucer, and the other ministers. He did not succeed, but, in a letter to Farel, Calvin confessed that he lost his temper during the arguments.

Many letters passed between the two men, for though separated, Calvin and Farel continued to be close friends.

*

The blind preacher Coraud was often in John's thoughts. The man had recovered sufficiently from his sufferings to take up a pastorate in the little town of Orbe. Now came the news that he had died. The news caused John many weary days and nights of grief, not because a servant of God had finished his course, and received the Master's 'Well done', but because of the rumour that Coraud had been poisoned.

Mystery also surrounded the death in Italy of John's cousin Robert Olivétan. He was only thirty-two years old, and again there was the suspicion of death by poisoning.

The pastor in Strasbourg pondered deeply on these events. Coraud, who had shared his labours in Geneva, and Olivétan, who, years earlier in Paris, had taught him something of the reformed faith – both were gone! They had died, it seemed, not a natural death as other men, but as martyrs for the Protestant cause.

IX
CALVIN AND THE CARDINAL

1539 was a critical year for the Protestant Church in Geneva. With new ministers taking the places of the expelled reformers, the citizens began to revert to their old way of life. Those who still wanted to uphold Calvin's ideals were soon in collision with the rest of the community. Bern made an attempt to establish its own political control over the city. Then, in the midst of the confused situation, the Pope tried to persuade the Genevans to return to the Roman Catholic faith. This important task was entrusted to Cardinal James Sadoleto, Bishop of Carpentras near Avignon. He was a devout, scholarly man, and more tolerant than some of his co-religionists.

Sadoleto therefore wrote a long and flattering letter to the people and senate of Geneva, saying, 'I have long loved your noble city ... but certain crafty men have crept in, turning you away from the Catholic Church. I ask you, is it more necessary for your salvation, and more pleasing to God, to believe and follow what the Catholic Church throughout the world has approved for more than 1500 years, or is it advisable to believe and follow the new ideas which sharp and cunning men have introduced within these last 25 years?'

The learned Cardinal continued his letter by depicting a Catholic and a Protestant giving an account of themselves before the judgment bar of God. As was to be expected, Sadoleto portrayed the Protestant as a man who held false doctrine.

And so the Genevans were invited to come back to the true fold.

However, the proud city by the Lake had no intention of putting itself under Rome's heavy yoke once more. A strongly-worded letter must be sent to Sadoleto, dealing carefully with the arguments he had propounded. But who would do the writing? A theologian was needed, but the Council could find no-one suited to the work. An appeal for help was made to Bern, and the revered Pastor Viret was approached, but he felt unable to take up the task. In these circumstances, said Bern, you must ask John Calvin to write the letter – no one is more capable than he.

John's friends had already sent him copies of Sadoleto's communication. The Strasbourg leaders urged him to accept the challenge. Calvin did so, and in six days completed the task. It was an amazing achievement, for his letter, written in Latin, contained some fifteen thousand words. It was a brilliant defence of Protestantism.

'With great reluctance I address you in terms of reproach . . . you soothe them by flattery . . . I cannot be silent,' Calvin said.

Then, using Sadoleto's method of dialogue and debate, he depicted a Protestant minister and a layman, also answering before God concerning their faith. With zeal and great earnestness, and drawing from his own spiritual experience, Calvin wrote convincingly. He upheld the authority of Holy Scripture, and maintained that the true Church was that in which the gospel was preached in its initial purity. It was not the Church of Rome!

The Cardinal was deeply disappointed. All his efforts had ended in failure, and what was most galling to him, the prestige of that heretic Calvin was enhanced!

*

As John continued his good work in Strasbourg, his friends there became concerned that he should find a wife. Martin Bucer, himself happily married, pleaded with him –

'Calvin, you ought to have a wife.'

John said he would consider the matter. When he had prayed about it, he decided that it would be a wise step, so in due course he wrote to Farel, describing the kind of bride he was looking for –

'Always keep in mind what I seek to find in her, for I am not one of those insane lovers smitten at first sight, with a fine figure. The only beauty which allures me is this – that she be virtuous and modest, dutiful and thrifty, patient, and likely to care about my health.'

Where would such a woman be found?

A certain high-born young lady, whose brother was a great admirer of Calvin, was recommended to him. Upon reflection, John saw that there could be certain disadvantages. Again he confided in Farel, –

'You understand, William, she would bring with her a large dowry, and this could be embarrassing to a poor minister like myself. I feel too, she might become dissatisfied with her humbler station in life. Then there is the difficulty of the language, for she does not speak French. I suggested that she learn it, but she was not enthusiastic.' This being the case, the negotiations were carried no further!

When another lady with admirable qualities was mentioned, Calvin promptly sent his own brother Antoine, who was with him in Strasbourg, to seek her out and bring her to him. With great expectation John awaited her arrival, only to be disappointed. There was obviously something about her which did not please him. Now he was in a dilemma. Having reached this stage, how could he say he did not wish to marry her? Fortunately, Antoine came to the rescue, and as gently and courteously as possible, informed the lady that Master John Calvin wished to be released from his obligation.

These experiences caused John to reconsider his position. Had he mistaken God's guidance? Would it, after all, be best for him to remain single?

While frequent letters were passing between Farel and himself upon the subject, the unexpected happened. Calvin fell in love with a member of his own congregation of French refugees. Idelette de Bure was a woman of sterling Christian character. She was beautiful too. The widow of Jean Stordeur of Liège, she had been left with two children, Jacques and Judith. This time there was no doubt whatever in Calvin's mind. Martin Bucer also urged him on. Idelette was the one whom God had chosen for him. They were married in August, 1540. Farel came over from Neuchâtel to perform the ceremony.

Calvin's earlier, somewhat cold description of his ideal bride, was now translated into the reality of warm love and partnership in his ministry. Idelette was good in the home, and cared greatly for his well-being. She visited the sick, and comforted the dying. She went with him on some of his journeys, and she entertained his friends. A woman of some force and individuality, John himself said that she was the best companion of his life. Their years together were very happy, though ill-health constantly dogged their pathway.

*

In the Spring of 1541, the deadly plague came to Strasbourg. John arranged for his wife to leave the city, and go to her brother's for safety, but he felt the parting very much.

'Day and night my wife has been constantly in my thoughts,' he told Farel.

When such an epidemic attacked a city, panic seized the population, and there was an immediate exodus from the stricken areas. But communities which were free from the terrible disease were reluctant to take in people who might have been in touch with it. Then, with the last hope of salvation shattered, dark despair took control. Certainly the authorities in a plague city were quick to take what measures they could to stop the disease from spreading. A ban was placed on every house containing a plague victim, and everyone who had come in contact with the patient was ordered to remain in isolation. Only specially authorized persons could carry food and other necessities to the house.

At night, the death carts rumbled along the streets, and the bodies of the dead were passed through the windows, and taken outside the city walls for burial in mass graves. It took a long time for a plague-ridden city to recover, and get back to normal.

*

While Strasbourg was battling with the pestilence, Emperor Charles V of Spain was waging another kind of war. The fierce armies of the Turks were threatening his Empire from the east, and he needed more troops. As head of the Holy Roman Empire, if only he could unite in their religion the Protestant and the Roman Catholic states of Germany, he thought they would fight side by side in his cause, and the hordes of infidels would be driven back.

'It is this matter of religion which weakens my war effort,' said Charles. He imagined he could end this schism in the Church, by organizing Conferences where differences in religion could be debated. So between 1539 and 1541, four Imperial Diets or Colloquies, as they were called, took place in Frankfurt, Hagenau, Worms and Ratisbon.

Rome sent its most eminent theologians, and the Protestants sent theirs, the chief spokesmen for the reformed faith being Philip Melanchthon and Martin Bucer.

At these important gatherings, Bucer wanted Calvin with him, and subsequently John Calvin

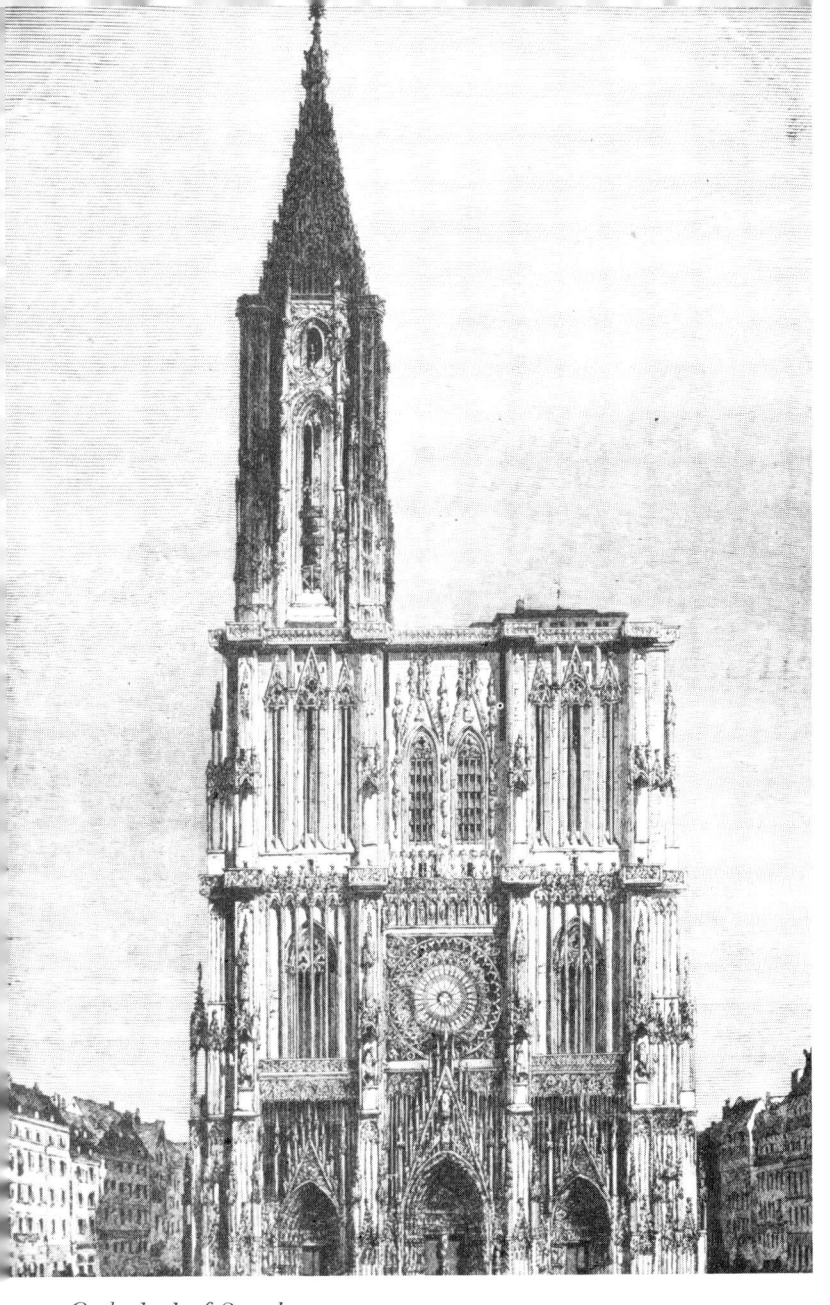

Cathedral of Strasburg

had the honour of being sent as a fully accredited delegate of the city of Strasbourg.

Genuine efforts were made to achieve agreement, but there were insurmountable difficulties. On vital points of doctrine neither side could give way, and the Conferences ended in deadlock. Although John found the constant travelling a hardship, and the long hours of debate wearying, there were some compensations, for he had the opportunity of meeting face to face the leading personalities of the day. He also was able to observe at first hand the progress of Protestantism in Germany, and to see for himself the way in which worship was conducted in the German churches. Calvin's acquaintance with Philip Melanchthon began at Frankfurt, and the friendship was cemented as the Conferences proceeded. Through Melanchthon he learned more about Martin Luther. This pleased him, for Calvin held Luther in high esteem.

The great debates at last were over, and John was on his way home. The plague was still raging in Strasbourg, and the thought of it distressed him. He was troubled too, by another, very personal problem which demanded a decision. He was being pressed to go back to Geneva, to resume his work there. But Calvin did not want to go!

X
GENEVA CALLS AGAIN

In the autumn of 1540, it was boldly affirmed by Geneva's Councils, that only Calvin's firm hand could restore peace to the troubled city. Only he could build up and strengthen the life and organization of the Protestant Church. Geneva was a strategic centre of the evangelical faith, but what was the Church doing to spread the gospel?

The Councils decided to invite Calvin back.

It was an important step, especially as a significant event took place in Rome at about the same time. In September, 1540, Ignatius Loyola knelt at the feet of Pope Paul III, and received the papal approval of his new Order – the Society of Jesus. Very soon the Jesuits, as members of the Order were called, would travel throughout Europe, and propagate the Roman Catholic faith with missionary zeal. If Rome needed Ignatius Loyola, then certainly Geneva must have John Calvin. So Geneva's messengers arrived in Strasbourg in search of 'the man in the black cloak,' but he was not there.

'Master Calvin is at Worms, representing our city at the Imperial Diet,' the men were told.

The distance was great, but the matter was urgent. The messengers were used to hard riding, and they spurred their horses onwards. Arriving in Worms after many days of travel, they enquired the whereabouts of the French pastor's lodging-place. Meeting him therefore at his inn, they solemnly handed him a letter stamped with Geneva's official seal.

John cut the string with his girdle-knife and broke the wax, but his hands trembled slightly, and his pale face grew paler still. As he read the pressing invitation, addressed to 'Doctor Calvin, Minister of the Gospel,' he was deeply moved. The letter begged him to transfer himself to Geneva, and return to his old place and former ministry. It seemed almost unbelievable that they should ask him back after all that had happened. That the citizens should promise to behave themselves in such a manner that he would have no cause for regret, astonished him. The tears ran down his cheeks, and he buried his face in his hands.

The Strasbourg friends who were with him in Worms did not know what to say or do to help him. Never before had they seen their pastor in such distress.

When he had recovered a little, and was able to speak, he told them –

'The very thought of Geneva is agony to me. Geneva was my cross, and every day I suffered a thousand deaths. Of course I want to assist them – but how can I return?'

John knew he must make a decision, but fortunately at the moment he had good and valid reasons for delay. First, he must fulfil his Conference assignments, and then he must consult Strasbourg Council. Accordingly, he wrote to Geneva, postponing his decision.

The weeks and months rolled by, and he reached home after the final Ratisbon Conference with his mind still in a turmoil. Geneva's coat of arms bore the Latin inscription, 'Post Tenebras Spero Lucem' – After Darkness, I hope for Light – but light had not yet come to Calvin.

Letters poured in from many quarters, and friends were ready to offer advice. It seemed that on every side, Calvin was being pressed to return to Geneva, and was promised a wonderful welcome. While Strasbourg did not wish to lose its illustrious pastor, it declared it was willing to let him go, for the gospel's sake and the furtherance of God's kingdom.

Still the man hesitated. He appeared to be weighed down by the memory of the daily stress and strain and suffering he had endured in the past. He reasoned that having once gone to Geneva at the call of God, he would have remained there however hard the task, had he not been expelled. Therefore, was it right or necessary to go back at the present time? The argument seemed convincing, but suddenly it dawned upon

Calvin re-enters Geneva

him that he was simply making excuses. The real problem was his own unwillingness; he was complaining about suffering, yet Jesus had said, –

'If any man will come after me, let him deny himself, and take up his cross daily, and follow me.' (Luke 9.23)

In a completely new frame of mind, Calvin saw the danger of the Church of Geneva being left without adequate leadership, and becoming spiritually destitute. The path of duty stretched out before him. He was no longer in darkness, for God's guidance was as a light upon his way.

'I am not my own,' he said. 'I offer up my heart as a sacrifice to the Lord. I submit my will and my affections to the obedience of God.'

*

On September 13th, 1541, John Calvin entered Geneva for his second period of service. Would it last but a few weeks or months? He did not know. In fact it lasted for the rest of his life! There were demonstrations of enthusiastic joy when he arrived, and a token of appreciation in the gift of a beautiful, new black gown of finest cloth, lined with fur. A new pulpit, specially carved, had been installed in the Cathedral of St. Pierre. Senate and people alike rejoiced to have Calvin back.

The Councils had agreed that his stipend should be five hundred florins per annum. This would

THE MAN OF GENEVA

not make him a rich man, but it would be adequate, enabling him to live comfortably. He would have a rent-free furnished house, and a sufficient supply of corn and wine for his household.

Calvin naturally wished to have his wife with him as soon as possible. However, both of them had felt it advisable that she should wait at Strasbourg until things had settled into shape.

'We desire to have the honour of making the arrangements for Madam Calvin's journey,' the reformer was told by members of the Council. He readily agreed, so they sent a carriage drawn by two fine horses to bring Idelette to her new home.

In the summer of 1542 a son was born, but the baby lived only a few days. The parents were heart-broken. John wrote to his friend and colleague, pastor Viret,

'The Lord has certainly inflicted a severe and bitter wound, in the death of our baby son, but he is himself a Father, and knows best what is good for his children.'

John and Idelette Calvin had no other child and she was never really well again.

*

Many distinguished people called at Number Eleven, Rue des Chanoines, where Calvin lived. The house was in the very heart of the city, quite

GENEVA CALLS AGAIN

near to the Cathedral. The men of Geneva loved to relate, with numerous variations, the story of one famous visitor, none other, they said, than Cardinal Sadoleto himself. He happened to be passing through the city, and was overcome with curiosity to see just where the prince of the Protestants lived. Being fully acquainted with the magnificent houses of the prelates of Rome, Sadoleto expected that Calvin, now a man of considerable fame in the Protestant world, would live in a mansion, in luxury and splendour. He was astonished beyond measure when he looked up at the unimposing dwelling which was Calvin's home. He knocked, and waited. No servant in uniform answered the summons. Instead, Calvin himself opened the door, wearing his usual long black robe – no scarlet or purple, no flashing jewels, not even a cross!

The Cardinal was dumbfounded. Evidently, the tales which he had heard were really true – money and fame meant nothing to Master Calvin. He was invited inside, and was ushered into a room where the walls were lined with books right up to the ceiling. There was a step-ladder too, so that a volume could be taken from the highest shelf quite easily. There were open books on the table, and orderly piles of letters, together with an inkhorn and pens. The master's carved chair, and a stool or two, completed the furniture. The curtains

Cardinal Sadoleto visits Calvin

were of tapestry, and were drawn back to let in the sunlight.

The house had a garden sloping down to the city walls; the fragrance of herbs and flowers filled the air with sweetness, and John took a pride in pointing out to his visitor his favourite shrubs and plants.

Although much of his time was given to study and writing, John's home was not the kind of place where all activity had to be suspended or subdued while the master was at work, lest he should be disturbed. His step-daughter Judith lived with them, while his brother Antoine with wife and family lodged under the same roof. There was a constant coming and going of relatives and friends, and the sound of laughter and the patter of little feet was quite familiar at the pastor's dwelling.

*

With perseverance and zeal, Calvin concentrated on his work of making Geneva a truly Christian city. When he produced his *Ecclesiastical Ordinances*, every line was scrutinized by the Councils, who insisted on some modifications being made, for though they had invited Calvin back, they were determined to retain their power over the Church. The *Ordinances* were based very clearly on New Testament teaching, and were comprehensive in scope. They covered not only the weighty matters of doctrine, but also practical measures for visiting prisoners in gaol, as well as provisions for ministering to the sick members in their homes. It is noteworthy that Calvin's *Ordinances* gave to laymen a place of responsibility and authority in the Church, quite unknown in the Church of Rome.

At a later date, Calvin was able to persuade the Councils to pass laws designed to contribute to the physical health and safety of the citizens. It is surprising to find a sixteenth-century city prohibiting the dumping of garbage in the streets, and forbidding the lighting of a fire in a room where there was no chimney. Houses with balconies must have railings, for the protection of children, and landlords must have official permission to let their accommodation.

Such was the advanced thinking of Geneva, under Calvin's influence.

XI
CALVIN'S GROWING INFLUENCE

On a summer evening in 1553, a stranger arrived in Geneva, and found lodging at 'The Rose' tavern. He was a Spaniard, a physician, and also a theologian of considerable ability. He informed the landlord that his destination was Naples, and that he would be needing a boat to take him across the lake towards Zurich.

The next day being Sunday, he mingled with the crowds making their way to the Cathedral. After the service, two friends began an animated conversation,

'Did you notice that visitor in one of the back pews?'

'Yes, but why do you ask? We have many visitors in church these days.'

'Well,' explained the first man, 'I am sure I have seen that stranger in some other place. If I am not mistaken, he is Michael Servetus, who was sentenced to death for heresy by the city court of Vienne, near Lyons. It is said that he escaped from prison, so they burned his effigy, a straw-filled dummy, instead of burning him. That man is a pestilence! He is hated by Catholics and Protestants alike. Come, we must tell Calvin at once.'

As Calvin had already gone to his home, the

two men hurried to the familiar house in the Rue des Chanoines, to pass on the important information.

The Councils were alerted, and that very day Servetus was arrested.

Why this haste to apprehend a man who, to the casual observer, appeared to be an honest traveller spending a few days in Geneva before completing his journey?

Servetus held strange, unorthodox views about the doctrine of the Trinity. He did not believe in Jesus as the eternal Son of God, co-equal and co-eternal with God the Father and God the Holy Spirit. He had written letters and had published books, in which he explained his own beliefs.

Calvin felt that the honour of Christ was at stake, and believed that it would be a service to God and the Church, if the man was removed from Geneva as soon as possible, not by banishment, but by death.

The Spaniard was about the same age as Calvin, who in fact, had followed his career quite closely. There had been an exchange of letters and manuscripts, and Calvin had tried unsuccessfully to show Servetus the error of his doctrines.

The ecclesiastical tribune of Vienne requested that Servetus should be sent back to their city, but this was refused. Was not Geneva's Council qualified to deal with the matter? The trial, which

CALVIN'S GROWING INFLUENCE

therefore took place in Geneva, was a lengthy one. Sometimes, by order of the Council, the evidence for prosecution and defence was in writing, in Latin. Sometimes there was a face-to-face confrontation, with wordy battles. Servetus was very abusive. He did not expect to be sentenced to death, and felt very sure of himself. Seeing that the Libertines – loose-living men – had once more gained power in Geneva, and were plotting Calvin's downfall, the Spaniard was counting on their help. However, the Little Council decided to ask advice of Bern, Zurich, Basle and Schaffhausen, and when the replies came in, it was seen that each of the four Swiss cities denounced Servetus as a heretic and blasphemer, harmful to the Church. The Libertines saw at once that their hopes of freeing Servetus were greatly diminished.

*

When the Little Council gave its verdict there was a gasp of horror.

Michael Servetus was found guilty, and was sentenced to death by burning. Calvin implored the Council to substitute death by the axe, as being swifter and more merciful, but his request was brushed aside, and the condemned man was burned at the stake, on the hill called Champel on October 27th, 1553.

If Servetus had been put to death at Rome or

Calvin and Servetus before the Council

CALVIN'S GROWING INFLUENCE

Vienna, most probably the sad event would have been forgotten within a comparatively short time. That a man should be put to death because of his religious beliefs in the Protestant city of Geneva, came as a shock, and called forth a storm of criticism and controversy. Time itself has not removed the stain which this left on Calvin's reputation. But Calvin lived in an age when heresy was everywhere regarded as a crime to be punished by the State, and in the matter of Servetus, the government of Geneva, and Calvin himself, acted according to the laws of that age. In the standard civil law-book, it stated clearly that for the crime of denying the Trinity, the penalty was death.

350 years later, a group of Christians who held to the teaching of Calvin, gathered near the place where Servetus died. On October 27th, 1903, they erected 'a monument of expiation', with an inscription in French, bearing witness to the fact that freedom of conscience must be held fast, as a true principle of the gospel.

*

Great numbers of Protestant refugees found their way to Geneva, and among them were men of outstanding ability. John Knox, whose preaching was forceful and lively, had exercised a powerful ministry both in Scotland and in

THE MAN OF GENEVA

England, but he too, had to seek a place of safety on the Continent. Not that he was a stranger to privation and suffering, for he spent eighteen long months as a galley-slave, having been taken prisoner by the French, when they made their daring bid to capture certain men in St. Andrews, who were responsible for the death of David Beaton, a Roman Catholic Cardinal. Only the influence of the young king, Edward VI of England, at last had secured Knox's release. Then in 1553, came the death of the boy king, bringing Mary Tudor to the throne. During her reign no Protestant was safe.

Like so many others, Knox found his desired haven in Geneva. During his second stay in the city, he had his family with him. He was an ardent disciple of Calvin, and was appointed pastor of the English refugees. He held his services in the auditorium adjoining the Cathedral. Knox spoke of Geneva in glowing terms:

'Here exists the most perfect school of Christ since the days of the apostles.'

For three years he enjoyed fellowship with the Genevan pastors, and above all, with Calvin himself. Then in 1559, leading men in Scotland, having themselves embraced the reformed faith, sent a message to him.

'Come home,' they urged, 'and advance the Reformation in Scotland.'

CALVIN'S GROWING INFLUENCE

The Queen, who had earned for herself the title of 'bloody Mary,' was dead. During the last three years of her reign, almost three hundred Protestants had been martyred, suffering a cruel death by burning. No mercy had been shown, and humble people who had let their light shine in obscurity had been ferreted out, and put to death, as well as spiritual leaders like Ridley, Latimer, Hooper and Cranmer.

When, therefore, Elizabeth I ascended the throne of England, a great sense of relief was felt by Protestants everywhere.

Returning home in response to his country's appeal, John Knox had the joy, in 1560, of seeing Protestantism established by order of Parliament, as the official religion of Scotland. The Presbyterian Church, as it came to be called, shared Calvin's doctrine and mode of Church government. Yet Calvin never visited England or Scotland during his many travels, and was dependent upon others for information about the religious situation in these islands. He had been deeply distressed by the news of Mary's reign of terror, and those who had escaped her fury and found refuge in Geneva, discovered in Calvin a true and understanding friend.

Though always busy with his pen, and with his preaching, and his many other engagements, Calvin's love for his own country never wavered.

THE MAN OF GENEVA

There was always within him an intense desire for the salvation of the people of France, and pastors and colporteurs working there, received a regular supply of French Bibles and Christian literature from Geneva. The missionary work was so successful that Calvin estimated in 1558 that a total of three hundred thousand people had turned from Rome to accept the evangelical faith, during the preceding years. Some of those had sealed their testimony with their blood.

Trained in Lausanne for the ministry of the gospel, five young Frenchmen, their studies completed, were on their way home. Immediately on crossing the border, they were arrested and thrown into prison. From the dungeon cell at Lyons, one of the men wrote to Calvin to let him know what had happened. When John received the letter, and read the tragic news, his face became grey with pain.

'My God,' he cried in agony, 'these fine young men in prison, and likely to die! O God, have mercy.'

Yet he marvelled that the letter was so full of faith and courage and trust in the Lord.

With all speed, Calvin set to work to secure their release, and an Appeal was made to the Parlement of Paris, while Bern petitioned the king of France. Again and again Calvin sent messages to the prisoners, assuring them of the

CALVIN'S GROWING INFLUENCE

prayers of God's people, and giving them words of comfort and encouragement. The Swiss churches used all their power and influence on behalf of the young preachers, but it was all in vain! After a year of waiting, the prisoners of Lyons were condemned to death by burning. Calvin sent them a farewell letter exhorting them to turn their minds heavenward. 'God will use your blood to seal his truth, and will not let a single drop of it be shed in vain,' he told them, and he signed himself 'Your humble brother, John Calvin.'

Calvin was regarded as the greatest theologian that the Reformation produced, but in spirit he, as an ordinary man, suffered with the martyrs, and was indeed their brother in the fiery trial.

On a fair May morning in 1553 the five prisoners were chained together, and led forth to die as they fulfilled their Lord's command:

'Be thou faithful unto death, and I will give thee a crown of life.' (Revelation 2:10.)

In spite of events like this, nothing could stop the advance of the gospel, and the Protestant congregations in France became an inspiring example to persecuted believers in every land.

It was about this time that the French Protestants began to be called Huguenots. It happened, so the story goes, that the people of Tours had noticed that the believers in that area were in the habit of meeting one another by night near the

Calvin preaching in the Cathedral of St. Pierre

gate of King Hugo – a legendary figure whose spirit was supposed to come out only in the dark. When therefore, a certain monk declared in a sermon, that as the Protestants apparently loved to gather in the dark, they must be kinsmen of King Hugo, and ought to be nicknamed Huguenots, the congregation was delighted with the idea. So the derisive title was attached to the Protestant community, and it stuck!

The story is a popular one, but it is more likely that the nickname 'Huguenots' is derived from some form of the German word *eidgenossen*, meaning 'confederates', with the first syllable perhaps being influenced by the French personal noun Hugues. The name probably originated, not in Tours, but in Geneva. But whatever was the true origin of their nick-name, these men had received the name of Christ and, like Calvin, had hearts on fire for the advance of the kingdom of God.

XII
THE CROWNING JOY

At last Calvin's dream became a reality. Geneva was a city transformed! The inhabitants, or at least many of them, turned from downright wickedness to out-and-out godliness. Violence and rioting disappeared, and it was safe to walk the streets at night. Men were more sober and hardworking, and the baneful influence of the Libertines was broken, since their leaders had fled to Bern.

The weaving industry, which Calvin had persuaded the Little Council to develop, was now flourishing, and it provided work for many of the refugees. Geneva's clock- and watch-making business was also winning renown, for the craftsmen were highly skilled. Some were immigrants from Florence, where they had been engaged in making beautifully embellished and expensive jewellery. This, however, did not find favour in the Reformation city, so the craftsmen used their skills in a new direction, and thus helped to make Switzerland famous for its watches.

Then came Calvin's crowning joy! It was the Geneva Academy. It was in fact, the first Protestant University in the world. At one time it had seemed so impossible, for Calvin was acquainted with no prince or prelate who would

THE CROWNING JOY

give his name and his money to such a project. Geneva was not a wealthy city, and though the population had grown to about twenty thousand, one-third of the inhabitants were refugees, who, when they were first given sanctuary, possessed little but the clothes they stood up in. Yet as soon as the Little Council granted permission for a site to be selected for the proposed college, it aroused remarkable interest and enthusiasm.

The poor, perhaps, could give only one coin, but successful business men could contribute liberally – and they did! In six months more than ten thousand florins were collected. While lawyers suggested to their wealthy clients that the Geneva Academy was worthy of support, and their legacies would ensure its success in future years, it was the immediate response of the ordinary citizens which specially gladdened Calvin's heart. So the foundations were laid, and little by little the building went up.

Calvin had always believed in the necessity of a good education to fit a man for his life-work, and he determined that the Academy should provide a course of studies as complete and extensive as possible, with a curriculum ranging from secondary education to the study of medicine, law and theology. Above all, Calvin's aim was to equip men for the Christian ministry, and the Academy became the very centre of Protestant theology.

THE MAN OF GENEVA

Significantly, three Scripture texts were inscribed in Hebrew, Greek and Latin in the arched roof of the porch, reminding the scholars of the excellency of divine Wisdom.

The Professors were chosen with great care, but the nominations first had to be presented to the Little Council, and approved by that body.

Theodore Beza was appointed Rector of the Geneva Academy. A man of brilliant intellect, Beza was an ardent disciple and intimate friend of Calvin. He was devoted to Calvin's theology and shared the same ideals.

An impressive inauguration service having taken place in St. Pierre's, the Academy was formally opened in June 1559, and from the very beginning, was a great success.

For Calvin it was the culmination of his years of strenuous effort to set up a proper educational system in Geneva. When he arrived in the city in 1536 he learned that a new school project had been mooted, and the General Assembly, largely through Farel's influence, had voted that the education of the poor should be free, 'and that every one be bound to send his children to the school, and have them learn.' The school had Calvin's full support. It flourished for a time and then declined. Indeed, every step towards progress was thwarted by the Council's lack of money as well as lack of enthusiasm. The reformer's period of exile certainly retarded the work, and on his return to Geneva he found difficulty in getting masters, and ensuring that they were adequately paid.

Calvin's *Ordinances* of 1541 put renewed emphasis on the importance of both religious and secular education. The *Ordinances* stipulated that a children's catechism class should be held each Sunday at mid-day in each of the three parish churches. Moreover, a school-master and his assistants must be appointed to teach languages and the humanities. In Calvin's view, all arts and sciences were a preparation for theology, which he regarded as the crown of education.

In the founding of the Academy, Calvin reached his goal. Boys came from all over Europe to be enrolled. There were two main departments, the *schola privata*, (the Collège) and the *schola publica*, (the Academy).

The *schola privata* took students through seven classes or forms, each class being under a *regent* or master. The seventh or lowest class was taught to read in French and Latin. The sixth and fifth classes concentrated on grammar and exercises. The study of Greek began in the fourth class and continued in the third, while the second class was occupied with elementary logic. The top class consolidated the studies, and completed the whole course, thus preparing students for the Academy, the *schola publica* where all subjects were at University level. On enrolment each student was required to put his signature to the reformed confession of faith. The Academy bestowed no degrees, but awarded certificates when students had completed the courses. The prestige of the Academy was such, that within five years the number of students rose to one thousand in the *schola privata* and three hundred in the *schola publica*. This was an achievement beyond all expectations.

A much less spectacular, but not insignificant event took place in the same year, when Geneva decreed that a minister of the gospel should be appointed to open each Council Meeting with a reading from the Scripture, and prayer. So in church, in school and in government, the authority of the Word of God was acknowledged.

December 25th, 1559 was also a pleasing occasion for Calvin, for on that day the Council offered him The Freedom of the City. He was quite overwhelmed by the honour, and found it almost impossible to find words in which to express his appreciation and thanks.

John Calvin was now fifty years of age. He had accomplished much, but his achievements he attributed to the grace and help of God. That he was a man of indomitable spirit, none could deny, for he had triumphed over obstacles which to most men would have proved insurmountable. Not only, like the apostle Paul, did he have 'the care of all the churches', but, also like the apostle, he was handicapped by physical infirmity. From his youth, Calvin had scarcely lived a day without pain. He was subject to very severe headaches, was laid low by fevers, and was a victim to arthritis and gout. At times he was in agony with gall-stones, and in his closing years he showed all the signs of advanced tuberculosis. This was the man who had offered his services as hospital chaplain, when the plague had swept through Geneva! No wonder the Little Council had refused his request; it would have meant certain death, and the Council would not allow him to sacrifice himself in this way. Calvin was attended by the best physicians, but they could do little to help him, as medical knowledge was so limited in the sixteenth century.

Calvin's wife, his dear Idelette, had died in 1549, and he missed her loving care, and sweet companionship. Yet still he preached, and lectured and kept on writing. His eyes shone brightly in the shrunken face, and his mental powers were unabated. He had secretaries to take down his sermons and lectures, and most of his correspondence he dictated.

Addressing the Council for the last time

THE MAN OF GENEVA

In 1559 Calvin completed his fully revised and final edition of the *Institutes*. The fruit of a lifetime of Biblical study, it was his masterpiece, providing a complete system of Protestant theology. It now consisted of four large volumes, containing a total of eighty chapters. The work was translated into many languages, and its fame spread throughout the world.

Almost equally famous were Calvin's Bible Commentaries. Many of these verse-by-verse expositions of Holy Scriptures were first delivered in Latin to his theological students in the form of lectures. The complete set of Commentaries covered thirty books of the Old Testament, and every book of the New Testament, with the exception of Revelation. They have been a source of inspiration to all succeeding generations of students and preachers. Three hundred years after Calvin, the renowned Charles Haddon Spurgeon declared that the Commentaries were 'worth their weight in gold.'

To the very last, Calvin continued working, though he found it increasingly difficult to walk the short distance to St. Pierre's, or to the Academy. To make it easier for him to attend the Council Meetings at the Town Hall, the steps to the Council Chamber were replaced by a ramp, and staves were fitted to his chair so that he could be carried from his home by his friends. Confrontation with the Council was a thing of the past, and an atmosphere of reverence pervaded the Council Chamber, as members listened to his speeches.

*

Calvin died on May 27th, 1564. It was a Saturday evening, and the end came peacefully. The following afternoon the long funeral procession slowly followed the road to the cemetery. Ministers from the churches, professors from the Academy, and city councillors, mingled with the great company of ordinary people. The plain wooden coffin containing Calvin's earthly remains was lowered into the grave, and covered with soil. There were no orations, and no pomp or ceremony. They buried him in simple fashion in an unmarked grave, according to his expressed wishes. With no stone to indicate his last resting-place, the exact spot was soon forgotten. Yet Calvin's name lives on!

In the wonderful story of the Protestant Reformation the name of John Calvin is outstanding. God used many servants in the great work, and it is recognized that it was Martin Luther, that daring pioneer, who first blazed the trail. The efforts of other notable reformers caused the Reformation to spread and widen out into several distinctive streams, each giving allegiance to the basic principles of the Protestant faith.

THE CROWNING JOY

John Calvin is remembered, however, not only because he made Geneva famous as *the* Reformation city, but because he gave to the world, in his *Institutes*, an interpretation of the Christian religion so profound, as largely to shape certain aspects of the history of Europe and America in the centuries which followed.

Theologians are still digging deep into Calvin's books and finding precious treasure. Others discover in the writings of the reformer, 'some things hard to be understood,' and they are offended. Yet all Christians who value their Protestant heritage will pay tribute to the man who loved the Bible above all other books; who expounded it so fully, and preached the Word of God so faithfully – the man whose one aim in life was the glory of Christ and the spread of the gospel.